SAINT GABRIEL POSSENTI, PASSIONIST

GABRIELE CINGOLANI

Saint Gabriel Possenti, Passionist

A Young Man in Love

Translated from the Italian by S.B. Zak

(Photographs courtesy of *L'Eco di San Gabriele*)

ALBA·HOUSE   NEW·YORK

SOCIETY OF ST. PAUL, 2187 VICTORY BLVD., STATEN ISLAND, NEW YORK 10314

ST PAULS

Italian language edition published by Edizioni Paoline, s.r.l., Cinisello Balsamo (Milan),
Italy, under the title *Gabriele dell'Addolorata*.

Library of Congress Cataloging-in-Publication Data

Cingolani, Gabriele, 1940-.
  [Gabriele dell'Addolorata. English]
  Saint Gabriel Possenti, Passionist: a young man in love /
Gabriele Cingolani; translated from the Italian by S.B. Zak.
      p.   cm.
  ISBN 0-8189-0790-8
    1. Gabriel of Our Lady of Sorrows, Saint, 1838-1862.   2. Christian
saints — Italy — Biography.   3. Passionists — Italy —Biography.
  I. Title.
  BX4700.G2C5713   1997
  282'.092 — dc21   97-3129
  [B]   CIP

Produced and designed in the United States of America by the
Fathers and Brothers of the Society of St. Paul,
2187 Victory Boulevard, Staten Island, New York 10314,
as part of their communications apostolate.

ISBN: 0-8189-0790-8

Printing Information:

Current Printing - first digit   1   2   3   4   5   6   7   8   9   10

Year of Current Printing - first year shown

1997   1998   1999   2000   2001   2002   2003   2004   2005

Table of Contents

Youth, Love and a Smile

It happens to everyone at least once.

You discover inside yourself a surprising ability to be happy and to make others happy.

You fall in love.

Someone once said that only then do you really begin to live. Before that, you are not able to give yourself completely because you have not yet savored the real taste of things.

And then it is over; but it has made you a person. The longing and the nostalgia remain, but at the same time you are able to go on because you have learned what it means to be alive. You have understood that the meaning of life consists in loving and in being loved.

This is what happened to him, as was normal.

But there is a difference.

For him, the falling in love of his youth never ended. There was no time for it to end, because his life was fully spent in this context, ending in his twenty-fourth year. If he had lived longer, he too would have grown to other stages of psychological maturity; but falling in love is also a level of maturity, as valid as any other and very important for the effects that it leaves.

Herein lies the explanation of the popularity of Gabriel of Our Lady of Sorrows. In every event of his life he is seen as a young man in love. At first thirsting for love and then overflowing with it. Not so much love for a girl, although he came very close to that, but love of life and of all that life entails.

It is no wonder that people find him interesting and are attracted to him. Everything revolves around this one central aspect of existence. We are all looking for love, we are blinded by it and get drunk with it, we long for it and go running after it, seeing it as the only real opportunity for happiness.

Young people are counted first among its friends because they are experts in the freshness and hope of love. It is still an immature love, as it lacks clarity and experience, yet it is still love.

All saints are people who are in love, because they are people who are fulfilled. But love takes on different aspects according to the different stages of life. Gabriel is the saint of love in its most intense phase. His life ended while love was still song and poetry. For this reason, although he is a saint for everyone, as are all the saints, he is in a special way the saint for young people.

He faced life with the typical attitude of those who want to get more from it. Doting parents, a flock of brothers and sisters, the best schools in the bustling Spoleto of the mid 1800's. For his father, assessor of the city, and his Jesuit professors he was a source of pride. He was among the top students in school; he stood out among his friends; he was exceptional on the dance floor, gripping in his dramatic recitations, and a person that others wanted to be with. He succeeded at being perfect because he was in love with everything he did. Accustomed to feeling important, he wanted always the best.

But life also dealt him some tough blows that left him gasping for air. His mother's death, the death of two brothers and three sisters. A couple of times he became so ill that he barely escaped death himself. Someone else might have felt betrayed by life and have complained that it wasn't fair. Not Gabriel. Always and unrepentantly in love, he waited for the right thing to come along, putting off other things that also attracted him strongly.

But at eighteen years of age it was time to make a decision, otherwise he really would fall in love and the decision would have already been made for him.

He really did fall in love. Love at first sight, the kind that strikes you without leaving other possibilities or alternatives.

While arrangements were being made at home for the engagement party, someone else shot a fatal glance at him and carried off his affections.

Who could this irresistible beauty have been?

This spark became a fire that could no longer be extinguished. Every move and every word betrayed the state of mind of the young man now in love. He wanted it all and he wanted it now, because he could hardly wait to finally be there. He would get what he wanted, for it was a characteristic trait of those who were in love: they believed that all things were possible, and so they would set out with determination and get precisely what they wanted. He wanted to say all the prayers, make all the sacrifices, establish all the contacts in order to be certain that he would be able to give everything he possibly could to this love that drew him into itself like a whirlpool. Everything in life and in the world that was beautiful he wanted to make his own; he wanted to feel that he was in the very middle of all the love rising from every human heart on its way to the limitless love of God.

Those who knew him well said that he was a conflagration ablaze with love or a mixture of dough leavened with love. He spoke like kindling that burst into flame at the slightest touch of a spark: a thing never seen and beyond explanation. Until at last the fire consumed him.

At twenty-four years of age he was spent and could last no longer. This life had nothing more to offer him and could only serve now to lead into the life hereafter. As he departed this world, not only was he without regrets but he was impatient and eager to be quickly on his way. Never had he been so filled with life as in the moment that he greeted death. While most everyone takes leave of this world with tears of farewell, he left with a smile on his face.

This is how he remains recorded in history.

His adventure seemed so fascinating to us that we gave in to the desire to recount it anew.

We want to recount it to everyone, because to the degree that we are in love with life, to that degree life is worth living, and to that degree it is a success.

And we especially want to recount it to young people, so that in their need for love they will not be deceived.

In the first Italian edition we added the subtitle, "A Blitz in the Skies of Holiness." Like a jet his heart plowed through the heavenly heights taking him to his destination on a direct flight made in record time.

Now we present his story once again, this time with a second key to understanding it, a key that is a development of that first image: this second key — that of a young man in love. A life that was a success because it never came down from the high that comes from being in love.

The Author

The Layman

Chapter One

Family and Life

The eleventh son was born in Assisi on March 1, 1838. They named him Francis Joseph Vincent Pacific Rufinus, in keeping with the pompous character of the upper middle class. Sante Possenti and Agnes Frisciotti had been married for fifteen years and already had eleven children, two of which had died before reaching the age of three.

The following is a mini-biography of each child, from the oldest to the youngest.

Lawrence was born in 1826 and lived until the age of twenty-seven. He enrolled in the Municipal Guard of Spoleto, and then moved to Rome where he joined a Masonic sect. When he received orders to commit a murder, he decided to kill himself instead. This caused great pain to the family and always remained a strict family secret.

Paul lived twenty-one years (1827 - 1848). He studied in the Seminary for three years. He tried unsuccessfully to become a member of the government militia police (the "carabinieri") and a customs officer. During the first war for independence, he enlisted in the University Volunteer Corps which sought to defend the borders of the Papal States, but love of his country drew him and his companions into the battle to free Italy from Austrian control. He was the most restless member of the family and died in the hospital at Chioggia after an attack of acute indigestion brought on by a meal of eels.

Mary Louisa: her life lasted twenty-six years, 1829-1855, and she spent all of it at home where she took on the duties of mother to the younger children.

Teresa came into the world in 1830 and she lived for almost seventy years. She married a lawyer from Belforte in the Marches and moved with him from city to city. She had six children.

Lewis' life span was sixty-six years, 1831 - 1907; he became a Dominican. He asked permission to leave the community to take care of his elderly father. In the meantime a law had gone into effect which banned Religious Orders and Congregations, so he remained outside the community, working at the Cathedral of Terni, until his death.

Adele lived only nine years, 1833-1842.

Michael was the longest-lived of the family, reaching ninety-seven years of age, 1834 - 1931. He studied medicine at Rome and practiced as a doctor in different cities. Because of his sympathetic leanings in favor of the Italian Risorgimento movement, he had to leave the country temporarily. Like his father he became a widower and, at forty years of age, had to take care of six young children, from ages nine years down to one month. From beginning to end he followed his brother Francis' rise to canonized sainthood and popularity.

Henry's life span was sixty-two years, 1835 - 1897. A good priest, he became a Canon and Prior of the Cathedral of Terni, where he was famous for his devotion to Our Lady. His father Sante, old and alone, spent the last years of his life with him.

Francis was the newborn son whose life we will shortly examine in its every detail.

From the preceding list are missing the first two children — *Paul*, who was born in 1824 and died in 1827 (when the other Paul was born), and *Lewis*, who was born in 1825 and died in 1828 (three years before the birth of the other

Lewis); also missing are the last two children, who were born after Francis.

Vincent was the first of these two and came into the world in 1839. He lived as a bachelor to the age of forty-three, dying in 1882. He spent his life mostly helping his father as secretary and assistant.

Rose, born in 1841, was the last child and lived a short life of only seven months.

All together there were thirteen children in nineteen years of marriage.

But building a family does not mean just bearing children. Building a family also involves instilling values and being helpful to others outside the immediate family circle. The Possenti's succeeded in building a family above all because of their positive presence in Assisi, where the father was governor and the mother the shaper of strong personalities which, once having left home, would have an influence on society. Both in the house and outside the home, the Possenti's bore Christian witness and performed social services, being attentive to the poor and involved in cultural matters. While more than two thirds of the society of that day were illiterate, all of the Possenti children went to school. Life's trials and the difficulties of the times were accepted with strength of character; the Possenti's lent a helping hand to the needy and were honest and fair. They gladly accepted as many children as they were given. Having a large family was not yet a source of scandal nor did it yet give rise to insensitive comments alluding to carelessness or excess.

When another little boy was added to the list, the Possenti's had been in Assisi just a little over a year and the newborn baby was the first to be born in that city. What name could they give him? The choice had already been made, being practically obligatory: Francis. He was also named Francis in memory of his paternal grandfather who had just recently died at Terni. He was baptized the same day on which he was born, in the Cathedral of Saint Rufinus, just like another Francis, the son of Peter Di Bernardone, seven centuries earlier.

The environment was that of the average middle class Italian family of the mid 1800's. The children were sociable and sought to imitate one another; strict discipline was observed in the home. This was all the result of the parents: an endearing mother, who was able to produce beautiful harmonies from a band that sometimes had some dissonant notes, and a strict but kind father, who at least in the mornings and evenings found a way to leave his own mark on the children's upbringing.

Agnes Anne Mary Seraphina Frisciotti, the mother, was a native of the Marches, from the city of Civitanova, where she was born on April 7, 1801, to a local noble family. At twenty-two years of age, on May 13, 1823, she married Sante Possenti, at that time governor of the city. In nineteen years of marriage she gave birth thirteen times, although some of the children only lived a short time.

The wife of a Papal official, she knew how to balance her formal duties alongside her husband with her dedication to the family, where she also had the help of faithful domestic servants. Her husband and the children would remember her as being "extremely pious." In their home, there was a special room set aside where she kept a sculpture of the Pietà; she spent long hours of prayer in that room. With her own hand she wrote a small book of moral guidelines, with thoughts taken from here and there, on which she meditated every day. Her "Collected Prayers" contained thirty prayers and devotional practices which she went through daily. When she died, her husband, the oldest children and hired domestic helpers had to work long and hard in order to provide some kind of substitute for her character-building and organizational skills which had left their mark on every aspect of Possenti home life. She was an exceptional woman.

Sante Valentine Mark John Balthazar Possenti was born in Terni on June 18, 1791. He had completed his studies in Rome, and from age twenty-five to sixty-seven was an official of the Papal States as governor, delegate and city assessor. He was named to twenty-seven different posts in the Marches, Umbria, and Lazio; however, he did not always move and establish residence in each new post.

He was governor in Camerano, Marsciano, Matelica, Civitanova, Canemorto, San Ginesio, Valentano, Corinaldo, Cingoli, Albano, Assisi, Montalto and Poggio Mirteto. He was delegate in Macerata three times, in Ancona and Perugia twice, and once each in Camerino, Frosinone, Viterbo, Comarca, Ascoli Piceno and Rieti. He was city assessor in Spoleto where he concluded his career.

At thirty-two years of age he married Agnes Frisciotti, who left him a widower at age fifty-one. Many of his numerous transfers were made at his request, in order to have a higher salary, which was needed for the family, or for reasons of health. He had a profound sense of duty and was very close to his wife and children. He was a devout Christian but not fanatical. His son Michael would say that he was "very pious." In the morning, he did not receive visitors or leave his room until after an hour of meditation. Then he would go to Mass, sometimes with one of the children, and finally to the office. In the evening he had everyone gather around to pray the rosary, after which there would follow an evaluation of the day during which he would give reminders and instruction, a kind of homily. He too would often stop and pause before the statue of the Pietà that was in its own special room.

He watched the children grow up one by one, feeling that he was not only teacher, but also confidant and friend. He would have to undergo some very difficult trials both in faith and in health. Besides work-related problems due to the tumultuous political situation in his forty-two years of service between 1816 and 1858, he would also have many worries because of the children. Only five outlived him, so he was present at or learned of the death of eight of them: three at less than three years of age, one at nine years old, and four when they were in the fullness of their vigor, between twenty-one and twenty-six years old.

The ordeal that was by far most difficult for him was the loss of his "most beloved wife." In his important but still little known collection of letters it is clear that his faith gave him the strength to go on. In every event of his life he was able to see "the adorable will of God."

In 1858, at sixty-seven years of age with eyes that could barely see and ears that were practically deaf, he finally received his dismissal from office but remained in Spoleto until the city fell into the hands of the Piedmontese. After rejecting the idea of going to Rome, he returned to Terni, the city of his birth, where he was taken in by his son Henry. There he completed his days on April 5, 1872, at eighty-one years of age.

Francis cannot be understood without an understanding of this father and this mother, great builders of character and themselves people of firm faith.

Nonetheless not even this family was able to escape the mystery that marks the fate of every family. It does not always follow that from good parents there will come good children, nor that from mediocre parents there will necessarily come problem-laden children. It depends on the mystery of the person, where many influences besides that of the parents come together; and we cannot say which influences will have a greater impact on each person. In the Possenti family not everything went smoothly. There was the saint and the Mason, the pacifist and the revolutionary, yet each came from the same good parents. Just like today, in the same family there can be one child who is very involved in the parish and another who is strung out on drugs.

Chapter Two

When Things Cause Your Smile to Go

The birth of a brother and a sister right after him, and the death of two other sisters, and two or three family moves that bounced him around from one place to another, and his father's absence for a year, and his mother's passing away: when all these things happen within the first four years of life, there is cause enough to say that things have not gotten off to a good start. A child of that age is not able to think in these terms or express himself in this way, but that is exactly how things were for Francis and they must have had some lasting effect on him.

Francis had to spend his first year outside the home. Agnes, weak and already exhausted by so many pregnancies and births, no longer had enough milk for him, so they sent him to a wet nurse, as they had done previously and would have to do with other children. He was nursed by Mrs. Batori, sister of the priest who baptized him, Father Joseph; she was a buxom country girl of Petrignano, a stone's throw from Assisi. The environment there was simple but healthy. When they would go to visit the child, his parents noted that he was treated "with kindness and was kept clean."

After the year was over, his mother was finally able to bring him back home and satisfy her need to cuddle him. But once again she was noticeably pregnant with Vincent, child number twelve, who would be born in 1839.

Francis was surprised by new crying in the crib. His

own crying mixed with that of Vincent and he discovered what it meant to have a little baby brother and to be one of so many in the house. Nonetheless, his second year was happier: he had the company of brothers and sisters and was bounced on the knees of Mom and Dad. His parents, according to what his age would allow, started him off on the work of growing and molding his personality: he was taught the sign of the cross, prayers, and consideration of others even when he would like everything his way.

His name was difficult for a child still so small, so he was immediately given a nickname: "Frankie" ("Checchino"). That was how his family called him his whole life, and that is how we too will call him until new events take place.

In May of 1840, his father Sante was named governor of Montalto in the Marches, but he decided to go there without moving the whole family because he foresaw that his responsibilities there would be short-term. He brought with him only Michael and Teresa, six and ten years old respectively, who would at least give him some company.

The house thus became emptier with the absence of three important family members. Francis had fewer people to play with, but the more serious issue was the lack of a father figure, which was important in children of his age, helping them to develop a sense of security, of creative strength, and a sense of the future. But Agnes took care of this need also, making it so that the children did not feel the absence of their father in their formative years. She combined her protective kindness with the firmness that her children also needed to experience. She did not interfere with the happy and carefree moments that children have, but neither did she cut down on the time set aside for prayer and instruction.

The municipal building in which they lived continued to accommodate the merry vivaciousness of the Possenti children even if the governor was away. There was a "narrow and steep" staircase leading to their apartment where the children could easily trip and fall, and there was also an inner courtyard that served well as a playground. Francis always wanted to know what was going on, and an incident that would always leave a particular impression on him was when he would surprise his mother while she was alone at prayer; even the older children were intrigued by this trait of their mother. As pastor of her own little church, she fulfilled her duties as teacher above all by her own example.

In the meantime, the children's father returned to Assisi whenever he could in order to enjoy the merrymaking of his big family. By the end of the year, Agnes was once again expecting.

In April of 1841, Sante was named governor of Poggio Mirteto, in the region of Lazio. This time the whole family bid farewell to Assisi and left because the prospects seemed like they would be long-term. For the children the trip was one fun, joy-filled thrill after another; but for Agnes, who was in the final days of her pregnancy, it was difficult. In fact, just after they finished the trip, the last child was born, the thirteenth, whom they named Rose.

Sante's new position in Poggio Mirteto could be considered a promotion, since it was a first-rate post in the Papal delegation of Rieti, but their stay in Poggio Mirteto proved to be a disappointment and a lot of hard work for everyone. Sante was not able to find a satisfactory house for the family, the duties of governor in that agitated little town were taxing, and the humidity was detrimental to his health and that of his wife. He was so nervous and unhappy there that after five months he asked for and received a forty-day leave so that he could recover his health. While he was spending this period of recuperation in Terni, his home town, he received news that he had been named legal assessor of the Papal delegation in Spoleto. This was a less prestigious post, but the pay was the same. For the time being, Sante was satisfied.

Up to this point, Francis had been growing up in a perfectly normal way, despite the somewhat irregular rhythm of family life. He was now four years old and continued growing as life carried him along; he was neither better nor worse than the other children. The effects of the different events of his life up to this point went into his subconscious and it was too early to say what effect they would have. The acting out and the affection that he displayed were normal for a child of his age. He was no longer the youngest, as there was a little brother and a baby sister; therefore he was no longer the center of attention. Among his sisters, it seems that some special quality brought him closest to Mary Louisa, who was twelve years old and was becoming a young lady. Perhaps he felt closest to her because she let him play more, allowed him to get away with things, and had two braids that were great fun to pull at!

Sante received his nomination to Spoleto on November 21, 1841, but the family did not move until the end of November. Everyone climbed once more into the carriage, all except Rose, the newborn, who did not seem as though she would survive at all; she was left with the wet nurse who had taken care of her up till then.

The first few months in Spoleto saw three devastating events take place that deeply affected everyone's life.

On December 8, little Rose died in Poggio Mirteto. Probably none of the family was able to be with her because of the difficulty of the recent move to Spoleto. Her life had been like a little light that shone only uncertainly and waveringly in all the six and a half months that she lasted.

On January 26, 1842, Adele died suddenly, at nine years of age. A cerebral hemorrhage left her paralyzed and ended her life in just a few hours; she died without being aware of what was happening. The family's despair at being unable to do anything was overcome only by the acceptance that was made possible by faith.

For Agnes, all of this was too much. Not for her faith, which was able to deal with it and even grew stronger, but for her physical temperament, which was fragile. She had been pregnant too often in the last few years — three children in four years; she suffered anxiety because of her husband's dissatisfaction in the most recent stages of his career; their recent stay in Poggio Mirteto had probably been very hard on her, Sante would later maintain; she was grief-stricken at the successive loss of two of her four little girls, especially of Adele who had been very close to her and who had shown the affection and understanding of a mature woman. All of this wore down her constitution.

Her son Michael, the doctor, would later explain that the death of Adele saddened her "excessively." "It was a source of tremendous pain for her and after a few days she took ill with meningitis, which in seven days took her to the grave."

Her death was quick but not sudden. The family had time to realize that she was dying and to prepare themselves for the anguish of the inevitable.

We have word that "Francis was hugged and kissed by his mother just a few hours before her death." And like Francis, so too all the others: each one received their good-bye and was given a final word of advice from their mother who had brought them life by giving up her own. This testimony allows us to imagine the silent and tormented presence, dignified and strong, of husband and children gathered around the bed where she said her good-byes and took leave of them, fully aware and fully giving herself in faith.

Agnes died on February 9, 1842, two weeks after her little girl; she was not yet forty-two years old. Francis saw that his mother was lying on the bed and that she moved no longer; he understood that he would not have her kisses anymore, or her hugs that had protected him and filled him with happiness. For the next few days he noticed that at home the desire to laugh and play had disappeared from the faces of everyone. We can never really know the effect that this experience had on his boyhood soul.

Chapter Three

Make Room, I'm Here Too

He was sensible, sweet and a great sweet-talker, but also quarrelsome with his brothers and sisters, impulsive, and a bit unruly. At four years old, the basic structure of his character was already evident and showed itself with fair consistency.

Little by little the external signs of mourning diminished and then disappeared altogether, although the wound was deep and would always remain. Francis was left without a mother. The danger now was that, as his personality continued to develop, the maternal element would be missing, the element that instilled emotional warmth, openness and joy in living. Would the little boy grow up unbalanced because of this lack of affection? Would he become a bitter and spiteful man who was closed and insecure? That could happen, but his mother had already left her mark. And besides, Francis would develop his affective relationship with his sister Mary Louisa; his father would try to temper the severity of his corrections with gentleness; and the family's very good and capable governess Pacifica Cucchi would be like a mother to him and would become an integral part of the family in nurturing the children's growth.

Physically, Francis was dark, "a cute little dark-skinned boy," slender and quick. He had a good appetite and was somewhat energetic, which served him well when he was at play in the various games which he often initiated and led.

He was "the liveliest of all the children." He was a darling little boy, as children at that age generally are. When Mary Louisa and Pacifica dressed him to go out for a walk, to Mass or to some kind of reception, he looked just like "a little lamb all adorned with ribbons."

He was devout, but not to the point of exaggeration. He was very serious when he prayed, and this would impress others. He felt that prayer was something important because he had so often surprised his father and mother when they were at prayer. But if he had to choose between going to Mass and running about with his friends, he would definitely choose the latter.

Among the different pastimes he enjoyed, there was also the building of little altars, as was common among the children of families who practiced their faith. He would build them and then officiate at them very seriously together with his brothers Vincent, Henry and Michael, while Mary Louisa would be the lone representative of the congregation.

In Spoleto, Sante had rented a ten-room apartment in the upper part of the city, on the Via della Trattoria. A very short distance away was the Ancaiani Palace, where the apostolic delegation had its headquarters; consequently, his office as legal assessor was also located there. Nearby were the Montani Palace, which housed the tribunal where he would also have appointments, and the Palace of the Genga, where the Brothers of the Christian Schools taught.

When he was six, in 1844, Francis began elementary school with the Christian Brothers. In those days, private schools of this type, given in trust by the city or the Bishop, were the only means for receiving formal instruction. In fact, before the State was able to provide the various social services on a general basis, they were all provided by religious organizations.

Francis now began his first educational experience outside the home. Having Religious Brothers as teachers meant not only learning to read and write, or studying grammar, arithmetic, history and geography, but also learning to pray and to assimilate Christian concepts of living. The Christian Brothers used the "La Salle" teaching method, which they had received from their founder, Saint John Baptist de La Salle.

This method aimed at basing life on piety and devotion, on horror of sin, and on devotion to Our Lady, to whom children are particularly open. The formation that Francis had received in the home was consolidated and developed in school, as was the foundation and orientation of his future. He proved immediately to be intelligent and alert. He was among the first in his class; this fact is also attested to by an arithmetic and geography test that we have from his early school days.

On June 1, 1846, he received the sacrament of Confirmation in the Church of Saint Gregory, from the Diocesan Bishop John Sabbioni. He was eight years old and had been prepared for this moment by his catechism lessons, and by an increase in his prayer and in his efforts to be good. We have no indications of particular influences of this experience on his life. Perhaps his awareness of the poor can be traced back to this period. At home he always saw that the poor were given special attention, but now he began to have personal contact with them, collecting items to distribute to them and sometimes giving up his lunch for them.

For the most part, he was well-behaved at home. He was faithful to prayer and to his father's advice as much as he was able, but he could still be bad sometimes. In general, he managed to get his own way in things, because it was not difficult for him to win over his father or his siblings with his ability to plead and beseech. But when he did not get his way, he would become very stubborn and would not budge. He stamped his feet and got angry: with Pacifica he acted as if he were the young master in order to make her give in; with his brothers, he screamed loudly to get his way. But his was a fire of straw. With his father for example, when

Sante's good nature started to peek through after a few minutes, and if he sensed that the moment was right, he threw himself about his neck with sweet entreaties and asked for forgiveness. His father, who had a weakness for him, was ready to forgive him but would act stern and would say that he wanted to see actions not just hear words. Francis' tendency to anger worried Sante, but he was reassured when he spoke to his son's teachers. They explained that there was no need for fear. The boy was becoming aware of his own personality; basically he was good.

Among his schoolmates he showed the characteristics of someone who came from a big family. He was sociable, connected with everyone, organized games, and was very popular. He would sometimes get into trouble because of his inability to accept being second, but only rarely.

While the boys went to school with the Christian Brothers, the girls went to the Pious Sisters. The rumor spread that there was a girl with six fingers on her right hand, and Frankie with some of his classmates was always curious to see her when she passed by.

He liked to go for walks with his brothers. They were generally accompanied by one of the servants, but sometimes they went out by themselves. Once, at Pontebari, in the Spoleto countryside, they met a peasant who was leading a horse with a pony alongside it. Here was a golden opportunity to go and poke the little horse! Frankie knew that he shouldn't, but he did anyway and the pony delivered a couple of kicks to his chest, throwing him across the road. He had the air knocked out of him for a few moments, but fortunately there were no visible bruises.

Another time, they got permission to walk through the woods of the Franciscans. Francis picked up a stone and threw it at a blackbird that was singing while perched on the branch of an oak tree. He knocked the bird to the ground, but it was still alive and he brought it home, happy to have something new and exciting to play with.

In 1845, Teresa returned to the family after being away at boarding school in Cingoli, where she had remained after going with her father to Montalto in 1840. She was now a young lady of fifteen, and for Francis she was like a new discovery, since they were together for only a few months when he was two years old.

In October of 1848, the news of Paul's death in a hospital of Chioggia arrived. Francis was ten years old and the talk of death was heard once more in the house, opening old wounds that had not yet healed. The pain could be seen above all on Sante's face. Francis was beginning to think, although he did not understand it much, that these things happened because of the "adorable will of God," since that was what he heard his father say, and he learned even at school. Death had become one of the threads of his life, like prayer, school, games and relationships. He was now ten years old and his life was no longer carefree.

As elementary school came to an end, it was evident that he had taken a step toward maturity. He was more reflective; at home and in church he participated in prayer without fuss and evasion. The churches he attended were: Saint Ansano, his parish; the ones run by the Oratorian Fathers and by the Servites; and the cathedral which was also the center for Marian devotion in Spoleto. Under the influence of those responsible for his education, both in the home and outside, his devotion became focused more and more on the Crucified Lord and Our Lady of Sorrows.

Chapter Four

The Hard Work of Growing Up

Completely normal. That is the title that can be given to Francis' infancy and adolescence. What we are saying about him here would not be worth setting in writing if it were not for what would happen later.

Adolescence is usually marked by the contradictions that are typical of that transitional phase of life.

Having completed his elementary studies, he continued to study at home unenthusiastically, occasionally with the help of others. In June of 1850 the Jesuits, who had been expelled during the unrest of 1846, reopened their school in Spoleto. In November Francis Possenti enrolled in the prestigious school and began his humanities studies there, which included what today would be considered middle and high school specializing in classical studies. He was almost thirteen years old and was entering a more adult and committed phase of life.

Spoleto of the mid-nineteenth century was full of an intense social, cultural and religious vitality, in spite of the general political situation of that period, which often created difficulties for the city and for all of Italy. It had a population of six thousand and counted some sixty large buildings and palatial homes, seventy churches and oratories, and seven parishes; it was a city on an eminently human scale where it was easy to meet others. Only those in the highest echelons of society were concerned with the political movements that were coursing up and down the peninsula; the upper class organized and attended cultural events that allowed them to show themselves off and which helped facilitate contact between their families. Their children paraded about and met each other while they were out on walks, while they were attending academies, dances, the theater or church. The boys had the added diversion of the hunt. The common people worked as tillers of the soil and as artisans; they got together in the marketplace, at festive celebrations and feastday masses. By and large, they had to be content with leisure activities at home with family and friends.

Religious fervor was evident in the many churches, confraternity groups, celebrations, popular devotions, and by the abundance of clergy. Besides many priests, there were the Conventuals Minor, the Observants Minor, the Minors Reformed, Capuchins, Jesuits, Redemptorists, Servites, Dominicans, Oratorians, Augustinians, Brothers of the Christian Schools. With regard to women Religious, there were Poor Clares, Augustinian, Benedictine and Servite Nuns, as well as Franciscan Sisters, the Sisterhood of the Child Jesus and Pious Sisters Filippini.

It is in this context that Francis made his entrance into the heart of life and culture. He had been born in Assisi, but his personality and formation were taking on the characteristics of Spoleto. As far as the rest of life was concerned, he would carry with him what he was learning here.

As he began secondary school with the Jesuits, his nineteen-year-old brother Lewis made his religious profession as a Dominican in Perugia and remained there to continue his studies. Michael, on the other hand, was still at home and attended the same school as Francis. Later, Michael would recall that in the mornings they "would have breakfast together and then go running off to school."

Francis' First Holy Communion can be dated to the beginning of his secondary school days. The Jesuits celebrated First Holy Communion on the feast of Saint Aloysius

Gonzaga, June 21. Therefore, Francis must have made his First Holy Communion on that date also, perhaps in the year 1851. In this period he was diligent and fervent in receiving the sacraments, attending Mass and visiting the Blessed Sacrament. At that time, however, it was still unthinkable to receive Communion more than two or three times a week.

The change of teachers and subject material brought no difficulties for Francis. He continued to do very well; studies for him were no problem. He was already getting good grades in Italian and Latin, and in the awards ceremony at the end of his first year he just missed earning first prize in both subjects.

At home, his influence with his father was increasing. Sante allowed himself to be swayed by Francis, who would intercede to spare his brothers some of the paternal nagging, to save them from some punishment, or to have them forgiven for some prank. His brothers saw him as the "mediator" and the "peacemaker of the family." He did not give up his independent ways or the right to get even if anyone tried to restrict his freedom, but he also knew how to be obedient and yielding. If there was some problem with his not being submissive enough, it lay in relation to his brothers, and not to his father whom he respected and loved deeply.

A good heart cannot be untrue to itself. One September morning while they were on their way to school, Michael saw Francis go off to a poor man and give him the "two or three coins" that he had managed to save. It was everything he had, because their father only rarely gave them money. There were recurring quarrels with Pacifica when she reminded him that he should be moderate in giving. But he insisted that even his father wanted them to be generous with the poor.

The carefree pleasures of young childhood were followed now by the more diverse activities of adolescence. Hunting, the only sport practiced at that time, caught his attention and attracted him because it gave him a sense of adventure and resourcefulness. He went hunting with his brothers, generally using birdlime and decoys. He was very good at imitating bird calls. Attracted by his imitations, birds came to the decoy and perched on sticks covered with birdlime. Sometimes his brothers also used a rifle, but he was not allowed to handle it because he was under-age.

During the day there were hunting trips into the country with his brothers and friends; at night there were evening outings for parties and get-togethers at the houses of friends, or for going to the theater. In such cases, he would get all cleaned up and would dress himself up just right, down to the smallest detail. Pacifica and Mary Louisa watched him grow with pride and some anxiety. They had everything ready for him, clothes all starched and pressed, shoes polished to a mirror-finish. He was already known as "a fashion plate." If the parties he went to ended with a dance, he felt a special tingling all over. He entered into the music as if transported to a far away place and his body itself became part of the song.

With his friends, he also enjoyed card games; these were a highly developed form of entertainment of that day. These games relaxed Francis and whetted his competitive spirit differently from other activities.

When there was some important engagement that would last into the night, the boys always went with Sante. But for afternoon get-togethers, birthdays and other things where the young people just wanted to be among themselves, they went unaccompanied with the understanding that they were to be back home by a pre-established time. Once, Michael and Francis were late in returning home because the friend they had gone to see offered them a special wine that made Francis sick. Was it a simple upset stomach or had Francis had too much to drink? In any event, the boys were out past the established curfew time, and Sante considered this a serious transgression. Michael was the one who got the brunt of the punishment because he was the older one and, consequently, the more responsible. For the time being, both of them were sent to bed without supper and without the possibility of explanations. Early the next morning, Francis had to put on all his charm with his father to make him accept the boys' version of what happened and to calm the storm that was preparing to blow.

1852 was a crucial year in Francis' adolescence. He was fourteen years old and the changes of puberty played havoc on his equilibrium, which was now more delicate than ever. He went through times when he was anxious, irritable and nervous, moments during which everything became difficult for him: studying, praying, being obedient, getting along with his brothers. He was not always able to control himself and his displays of anger were more violent now that he was older. Sometimes when he was reprimanded, even at school, he greatly overreacted and just dropped everything, slamming the door behind him as he disappeared. And then he easily broke down, even to the point of bursting into tears.

These normal manifestations of his evolving character seemed excessive even to Sante, who was experienced with children. So much was Sante concerned by them that he decided that it would be best to send Francis off to a seminary. This would make things more difficult for Sante, because Francis helped him with his work, even though Michael was his official secretary. But Sante believed that it would be best if Francis had a more organized and systematic educational experience. Therefore, on September 23 he wrote to his nephew in Terni, Peter Possenti, asking him to check with the rector of the seminary to see if there might be room for Francis: "I would like to place my son Francis in your seminary. He is always getting into trouble and does not get along at all with his brothers and sisters. He does not tend to his studies, although he shows talent and demonstrates some inclination to become a priest."

During this period Sante was also upset because of his son Lawrence. Lawrence had been traveling back and forth between Rome, where he attended the university, and Spoleto, where he was enrolled in the Municipal Guard; one day without prior warning, he said good-bye to everyone and left permanently for the capital. Henry was still at home; since he studied at the seminary and was already seventeen years old, Sante had him oversee his brothers' studies. Henry told how Francis, during this difficult period, seemed particularly unrestrained in giving himself to fun and games, and in looking for carefree company. Even his Jesuit teachers made an attempt to deter him "from the path of vanity which he seemed to be heading down with excess." The plan to send Francis off to seminary boarding school did not work out. Hoping that he would pay more heed to an outside tutor, Sante asked his friend Philip Fabi to help out occasionally; he would assist the boys with their studies and with the refinement of their manners.

As a result of this tormented period, Francis' school report for the year 1852 showed a drop, a sign that he was applying himself less to his studies, or that it was just more difficult for him to do so. In the awards ceremony at the end of the academic year he got only an "honorable mention."

This behavior did not sum up Francis' life at this point; it was only one side of his ups and downs, the other side included his efforts to pray regularly, receive the sacraments faithfully and keep his devotional practices up. As with all the Jesuits' students, he was enrolled in the Sodality of Mary. He went to the meetings and was the favorite choice to read the lessons because of his beautiful voice. At home, he continued to take moments for reflection before the statue of the Pietà, as he had learned from his mother and as his father's example still reminded him to do. He did the same in the Church of Saint Luke where an image of Our Lady of Sorrows was prominently displayed; this image made quite an impression on him. He would stop for prayer and reflection also in the other churches that he went to with family and classmates, or just by himself.

His classmate Paul Bonaccia surprised him once in one of these churches where he was sitting with his chin in his hands and his eyes wet with tears. Francis realized that something unusual was happening to him. He felt an inner drive to do good things, but he was not able to follow through with it; he also felt certain of life's urges that he could not resist. Who knows what was going on inside of him? Instability was the clearest distinguishing mark of this period. One moment he was all devotion and piety, the next pure vanity; now all study and commitment, then complete boredom and listlessness. Although he may yet have lacked sufficient affective awareness, he had to deal with the stirrings that were the prelude to young adulthood. But he did not let himself be overcome by them. One day his friend Giovanetti found him upset and angry with a sharp pruning knife in hand; this knife, which he had used to chase away a friend who had made indecent proposals to him, was a sign that he did not always get angry for no reason at all, but that he would also get angry to defend values.

In 1853, some events took place in the family that affected him profoundly. In February, there arrived from Rome the news of his brother Lawrence's death. Further reports came, first specifying that he had died a violent death, then that he had committed suicide, the motivation of which, people were led to believe, was a failed romance.

In September Teresa got married in the parish church of Saint Ansano; she wed the lawyer Pellegrino Pellegrini, who was from the Marches and was Fiscal Procurator of Spoleto at the time. Francis' brother Lewis, the Dominican, was transferred from Perugia to Lucca where he would finish his theological studies, be ordained a priest and from where he would then be sent to work in Livorno.

There were now empty rooms in the big Possenti house in Spoleto, and more than that, the psychological ties that bound the family together were starting to be broken. Of the formerly large and noisy household there now remained with

Francis only Michael, Vincent and Mary Louisa, plus Henry who came and went as his seminary schedule allowed.

As if making peace with all this, Francis felt more stable and serene, with a certain equilibrium that made him more at ease with himself and able to get along better with others. His performance in school also improved greatly. In the final scholastic competitions he got first prize in Latin and second in Italian and religion. For piety, modesty and diligence he received "honorable mention."

Chapter Five

When Your Heart ...

A young man who was promising in every way. This was Francis at fifteen and sixteen years old: the age when friendships and attractions start to turn into love, when life projects start to take shape, and when there is an eagerness to succeed at all costs. None of this was lacking in Francis' life, even if there would remain deep inside of him an unresolved restlessness that we will look at soon.

There is no fixed calendar date that we can establish as the end of his adolescence and the beginning of young adulthood, but it had happened: Francis was straddling the area between these two periods of life and gradually entered fully into the latter.

October of 1854 was perhaps the last period of adolescent melancholia. On vacation in Ferentillo (in the province of Terni), he was bored to death and was constantly bothering his cousin Peter of Terni with letters and messengers asking Peter to send him the hunting equipment — the only way he saw to kill time. That same autumn, he became his father's sole secretary because Michael had left home to study medicine at the University of Rome. This was a job that earned him a lot of respect, but it was also full of responsibilities; it meant that in his going about, he had to be on his best behavior. As part of his job he read to Sante, whose eyesight had become very poor; he read him the Official Gazette, wrote letters for him, accompanied him on walks. They took an afternoon walk almost every day, and it always included a stop of at least fifteen minutes at the Church of Saint Luke to pray before the image of Our Lady of Sorrows.

The sharing between father and son became more intimate. Sante, who was now sixty-three years old and was entering old age, experienced the most satisfying moments of his fatherhood with this son who was making fine progress in moving forward into young adulthood. He saw himself in Francis and felt that Francis' life was an extension of his own; he would have liked to give him the best he had to give, including his career. Francis was obedient and helpful, he grew in admiration for his father but also in his own desire for future independence. He admired above all his father's honesty and sterling character. One day, a nice big fish that Pacifica had prepared as a real culinary masterpiece was brought to the table and the whole dining room was filled with the appetizing aroma. Sante, suspicious of something, asked where the fish had come from. When he was told that it was a gift, he ordered that it be removed and given to the poor, because the man who had given it to them had a case pending before Sante. The watering mouths remained, but good nourishment is also provided by good example.

In his role as collaborator, Francis sometimes received clients and gave their problems the first scrutiny. One time, a lady wanted to put in a good word for her son whose case was being heard. Francis had her explain what the case was about and, at the end of the explanation, commented that it was really a serious matter and that there was little she could do to help her son. Quoting a piece of popular wisdom, the woman rationalized saying that "not a leaf stirs unless God wills it." Sure, replied Francis, but that does not mean that God himself is responsible for your son's shady business! Then he gave a little lesson in catechism and tried to set the woman's thinking straight.

His humanities studies were bringing about changes

within him and were making him feel more ready than ever to take on life.

In the still semi-clandestine culture of that time, however, one of history's biggest crises of thought was ready to break out: the Enlightenment. The Enlightenment taught that everything from the past was to be thrown out; this philosophy was already fomenting rebellion against every kind of dogmatic absolutism. Taken together, rationalism, enlightenment, subjectivism, critical philosophy, dialectic materialism, were all launching an attack against the patrimony of faith which, up till then, had been unassailable.

Francis found himself in the midst of the turmoil of this historical period. Many of his classmates would be attracted to these different patterns of thought and would remain entangled in their consequent political manifestations. But not Francis. The Jesuits were very thorough. They worked at making students develop their imagination, their sensibilities and their mind so that they would be able to reflect on themselves; they also encouraged discussions during academic exercises so that the students would be able to express themselves and engage in debate. In the literature classes, they emphasized the classics because these provided a basis for Christianity; in philosophy they studied in depth Christian authors who provided the framework for critical thought. Students who had completed their studies with the Jesuits were well trained in the use of the intellect and will, without questioning the primacy of faith.

Scholastic formation was integrated with religious formation, which the Jesuits saw to especially in the Sodality of Mary. Here they made use of the same structure that was used at school. It was with this integrated formation that the characteristic Ignatian spirituality was instilled, the spirituality founded on the person of Christ and on the spiritual combat that was necessary if one were to really follow him. The enemies to be engaged in battle were the world, the flesh and the devil; the end to be attained was pure love of God. The whole was permeated through and through with apostolic zeal and sustained by pious practices that culminated in devotion to Mary.

As had been true of his earlier schooling with the La Salle method of the Christian Brothers, so too this spiritual infrastructure given by the Jesuits was fundamental in building Francis' internal character. He always carried the imprint of these formators and was always grateful to them. With the help of these teachers he definitively assimilated a sense of God in history and in concrete life. Whenever he wrote anything, he headed the paper with the Jesuit motto "AMDG" ("*Ad Maiorem Dei Gloriam,*" meaning "to the greater glory of God"). In the following years, when he heard of the adverse turn of events that would come to cause the Jesuits much trouble, he would not tolerate that anyone speak ill of them.

A confirmation of this was the mystery, still unexplained, surrounding Francis' request in 1854 to become a Jesuit. His request was accepted, but he never entered the Order. Could it have been that life had distracted him from this notion, or had something dissuaded the circumspect religious Superiors from wanting to get involved with the son of an Assessor of the Papal States?

It would be interesting to know what Francis and his father thought of the unification of Italy, but there are no sources providing us with this information. Francis' participation in cultural events was limited to school, drawing rooms and the reading he did outside of classes. His school itself was well insulated and protected from the external tumult, the drawing rooms were those of the well-to-do who moved about in government circles, and for reading, books were chosen that countered the reactionary and pagan mood of the times with Christian values. Francis would not have read more than Manzoni, Grossi, Tommaseo and Bresciani.

His personality also bore the imprint of 19th-century romanticism, but classicism had left the stronger mark on him. He learned more, for example, from reading Latin texts or translations from Latin than from reading Italian novels. Among his own compositions that have come down to us, those in Latin are better than those in Italian. His inclination for classical studies over scientific studies was also evident, and he did not do poorly in philosophy either. In fact, in his two-year course of philosophical studies, he willingly agreed to copy over the notes of his professor, Father Charles Joseph Bompiani.

Francis was a part of the Jesuit cultural center of Spoleto and he had no trouble maintaining his place in this milieu. He actually did very well: he wrote first-rate essays; in the final exams he was always among those who received top awards; the professors were happy with him. He himself was satisfied with his studies, they gave him a feeling of fulfillment and made him confident about entering into adulthood.

In social circles he was equally successful. He passed his time more or less as before, but always with more refinement: hunting, drawing rooms, playing cards, going to dances, the theater, taking part in plays and school presentations where, as actor, he was able to move audiences to tears and bring them to their feet with applause. Nor was he unaffected by the charms of girls. He was experiencing all the joys of life. In drawing rooms he stimulated conversation, built relationships, shone brightly and was sociable; he was able to participate in serious conversations as well as make small talk: he was a young man "with whom you could enjoy yourself."

When it came to dancing, he had perfected his earlier amateurish whirling about the room and now had excellent, impeccable form. He would go dancing in public places, but from 1855 on he danced mostly in private homes, since there was a cholera epidemic, first in the area surrounding Spoleto, and then in Spoleto itself. He went especially to the houses of the Parenzi's, the Pianciani's and the Campello's. Francis was very popular and the life of the party at these social gatherings also, but here he was always under the watchful eye of Sante who kept him from going overboard. His father had him accept every invitation, either accompanying him himself or sending him off with others; for it was now time for Francis to enter fully into adult life, but Sante never let him go off alone. Without keeping him on a leash, he was able to push him forward and pull him back at the same time, even with just a brief glance, and Francis was not bothered in the least by this tie to his father.

He dressed in a manner that was obviously the latest style, either "from overseas or from beyond the mountains," as his friend Paul Bonaccia remarked. He did not tolerate even a crease that was out of place; he left behind a strong scent of cologne when he passed by; his hair was properly combed, parted and slicked into place. More to give himself a cool look than because of a bad habit, he decided to see what smoking was like. For some time there was the suspicion at home that he was smoking, because the rooms smelled of the tell-tale odor; and one evening when Michael was arriving from Rome to visit his family, he caught Francis out on the streets of Spoleto smoking. It was useless to deny it any longer.

Among his women friends there was one in particular to whom he made overtures: Mary, the youngest daughter of the lawyer Pennacchietti. She was a "virtuous girl who was fond of him." At least once, as far as we know, they went to the opera together, perhaps during the pre-Lenten carnival in 1855, when *Il Trovatore* was playing in Spoleto. Mary Louisa decided to go with her friend Mary Pennacchietti, and she invited Francis, giving him the job of reserving box seats for them. It is possible that Teresa, recently married but still in Spoleto, tagged along with them. And so everyone was at the show. "On that occasion, Francis was courteous and pleasant company for the young woman." That time, and probably others, they exchanged novels that they were reading.

Mary was fond of him, and he was pleasant and gentlemanly; so they went out together, after all, his heart was not made of stone.

Many years later, in 1908, Mary lived in Rome where she was the wife of a high army official. She was invited to "share helpful reflections from fifty-two years earlier on the Possenti boy of Spoleto" as she followed his beatification ceremony. It is too bad that none of those reflections have come down to us.

Up to this time, the strongest affective tie in Francis' life was with his sister Mary Louisa. His mother's passing away when he was very young prevented him from experiencing the full depth of that maternal bond, and his love for his father was something different. Mary Louisa, nine years older than he, had joined together in herself the aspects and influences of the feminine figure in Francis' psyche: for him, she was part mother, part sister, and part girlfriend all rolled into one. She was another determining factor in his life. Her life, taking the place of the mother who had died at too early an age, came and went in silence. We know practically nothing of her, only that she was regular in attending Mass and receiving Communion at the parish church, that Francis had great love for her, and that she died suddenly on June 7, 1855, while the Corpus Christi procession was passing through the streets of Spoleto. We have no precise information on the cause of her death. She was not well, but not even the doctor suspected that she would pass away so quickly; in fact, with the doctor's reassurance, Francis left her to participate in the Corpus Christi celebration, leading the procession as Cross-bearer. During the procession, someone came up to him telling him to return home quickly.

His eighteen-year-old heart was put under great stress by so many adverse events. Was happiness simply impossible? Never had a death been so difficult for Francis. Another piece of life disappeared, while his own life was still so young.

Chapter Six

Handsome and Thirsting for Life

Attractive, pleasant, kind and friendly. Full of life, joy and wit. Cheerful, playful, good-natured, smiling, jovial, clever and intelligent. Smooth, gentle, persuasive and very affectionate. Cordial, courteous and approachable. Generous, obliging and loving. Straightforward and sincere. Noble, dignified and distinguished. Sociable and good at making friends. Sensitive, refined, warm and tender. Docile, submissive and obedient. Dependable and zealous. Devout and pious. Good, sensible, precise, alert and shrewd, with a quick and capable mind. Talkative, with a nimble and able tongue, and a sonorous voice. Likeable. Handsome.

Also vain, ambitious, frivolous and worldly. Stubborn and unyielding. Quick-tempered, unpredictable, impetuous, harsh and impulsive. Fickle, unstable and inconstant. Independent, impatient and self-sufficient. He liked to enjoy himself, engage in conversation, go to the theater and dress colorfully.

These were the descriptions that came up in the reports on Francis' life as a young man. At this point in his life, his character, nature and body had a certain configuration such that we can give a brief overview. Many of the qualities reported here can be drawn from what we have already recounted. Some of them can be better documented. We are going to do that now.

A certain good-naturedness is always present in those

who are intelligent, unless they suffer from some abnormality. When he was engaged in conversation, Francis would often make some witty comment or clever remark that would catch everyone's attention. At the proper place and time he knew how to "embellish his talk with humor and wit" but never with "stupid or vulgar stories." He was very funny when telling jokes or recounting "humorous events." His sense of humor can be seen in the caricatures that he drew for his friends; his friend Giovannetti has preserved a sample for us: he would make use of huge bellies, enormous top hats and bold lines to exaggerate the particular traits of each person.

He knew how to take jokes when they were at his expense, and he was able to make up original jokes at the expense of others. His father wanted him to wear a top hat instead of his normal hat, because he thought it is more stylish. Some of his friends had fun poking at the hat and making it crooked on his head. One morning, Francis prepared some fun of his own, by putting in the hat some pins with their sharp points sticking out. Those who would have fun playing with his hat soon had the desire to play with it no longer.

His generosity was shown not only to the poor, but first and foremost to his own family. Once when all the boys who were still at home had gone on a hunting trip together, Michael badly cut his hand while using a knife to get some branches from a tree. Francis was the only one who jumped into action, running back to Spoleto to get a clean linen bandage. He was not able to find the doctor, however, and the pharmacist would not give him anything without a note from the doctor. He returned quickly to his wounded brother, having run a total of six miles, and was embarrassed that he had not been successful in his trip. But he was ready to return to town again if there was something else that might have proved useful. They took care of Michael's cut by applying pressure and dressing it as best they could. Michael would have the scar for the rest of his life.

Another time Teresa was upset because she had lost a jeweled pin while returning home after a party. Francis went out that very night with a lantern, taking Michael along with him, and retraced Teresa's path looking closely at every step until the pin was found and returned to its owner.

He even willingly gave to others the things that were most special to him. When he was finally able to get himself a watch, he hinted to his cousin Peter that it would have been very nice to have a watch chain that ran from his chest to the pocket where the watch was kept. Peter sent him a gold chain as a gift. Francis, greatly surprised by the generosity of the gift, showed it off for a bit but then gave it to his brothers. He tried to embellish his new straw hat with a ribbon of silk velvet. But since Pacifica was very fond of the ribbon, he gave it to her so she could use it as a belt.

The refinement of his character made him sensitive and considerate in his relationships. He was remembered as someone with "extraordinary sensitivity" and "a very sensitive heart full of love"; he was described as "affectionate, gentle and compassionate." Because of his gifts in this area, he was able to sense, adapt himself to, and influence the moods of others. To win the sympathy of others and get what he wanted, he knew how to maneuver, sweet-talk, and manipulate: wonderful traits that could also be very dangerous.

There is no question that he was very intelligent, but how could his shrewdness be explained? It was an aspect of his acute intelligence in relation to practical matters. People said that he could sense things "in the air" and was able to enjoy them if they were good or avoid them if they were bad. "He is so clever that no one ever succeeds in pulling the wool over his eyes!" Occasionally he may have been something of a schemer, but is that so bad?

It cannot be said, though, that he was without his defects. They come from the distortion of his positive traits, but there is no need to insist on certain negative behavior patterns of his youth. Francis will deeply regret the dances, his going to the theater, the novels, the card-playing, the meticulousness with which he dressed, and his carefree attitude — which in his case was not necessary. People today would not regret these things.

As a whole, the young man made a positive impression. "Attractive manners, pleasant features, a kindly bearing." Merely seeing him, made one want to strike up a conversation with him and to become friends with him.

If we had to put him into one of our modern psychological categories, we would say that he had a cyclothymic introverted character with a passionate secondary active emotional temperament. In fact, he had a tendency to be moody, showing great euphoria and optimism one moment, and falling into some deep depression the next.

His emotional traits were such that everything that was part of his humanity participated in the great attraction he felt for ideals. This made him sensitive to spiritual issues and, in group settings, it enabled him to find points of agreement amidst differences, which made him a good leader.

The active dimension of his personality enabled him to grasp the possible relation between the ideal and reality, and enabled him to be an achiever, overcoming obstacles. This was the dynamic of his independence and impulsiveness, his tenacity and perseverance, his honesty in his opinions and in his relationships, his pride and ambition, his consistency and balance, and his strong will to get what he wanted.

As concerns his secondary traits, although they too showed many primary characteristics, he knew how to reflect on things, allowing himself time alone in order to think, which was made easier by his prevalently speculative intelligence. He may have sometimes indulged in fantasies, but he was inventive and was also a capable planner. He followed through on projects and persevered in evaluating his interests and his own personal experiences; these were a source of learning for him. His many talents, because of their great variety, could sometimes come into conflict with one another, and he would not know which instinct to follow first or how far to take it before giving precedence to another aspect of this rich treasury upon which he could draw.

His passionate trait was expressed in the warm way he experienced everything. He could never be superficial for long, because he lived deeply the values and relationships with the people and events that concerned him, always with strong emotional attachment.

This was clearly the type of person Francis was, even though he was still growing and the structure of his thought, actions and style was not yet fully mature. Moreover, the typical characteristics themselves were always relative. The typology here was that of totality, which by its nature is never content to stop half-way. Prominent and notorious personalities usually belong to this personality type, the great saint or the great villain. To this same prototype belong Paul the Apostle, Peter the first Pope, Polycarp, Augustine and Teresa of Avila.

What about Francis' physical characteristics? He was good-looking. His external physique matched his interior beauty. "He had a handsome appearance." Dark complexion, tall and slender with a round or "roundish" face — "more round than oval"; dark brown hair with unruly curls, like those worn by the fashion-conscious of today, but he tamed his curls with gel and his hair was neatly parted down the middle. His eyes were round, dark, lively and filled with light: they were "full of life and very attractive"; "a bit large and enchanting"; "they looked like two stars and were very beautiful." Gentle pink lips that "continuously smiled." He had the beginnings of a beard that was still light peach fuzz. These were not descriptions given by his girlfriend, but by classmates and teachers. One day, in part because he felt that he was good-looking and in part because there happened to be a photographer in Spoleto, he wanted to have his photograph taken. At home, however, they discouraged him from doing so, having him put it off for another time. It is a pity that this "other time" never came.

His nose, lending itself to a nice, full profile, had unfortunately been the victim of an accident. One day, when he was running through the big house in Spoleto with his brothers, Henry suddenly closed the door behind him, and Francis was not able to stop in time. He ran into the door and broke his nose. After healing, it remained a little off-center, leaning slightly to the left. But one line that was off did not ruin the beauty of a face that was almost like that of an angel.

This was what Francis was like at eighteen years of age. He felt that he was overflowing and ready to explode, full of possibilities, eager to love and to have new paths open up before him; he had been made for life and joy. He loved everything that was beautiful: friendship, learning, entertainment, success, good feelings. He was loved and accepted. He was very much attracted by life and gave himself to it completely, without the slightest hesitation. And yet, something inside kept him from being fully satisfied, as if all this were not enough.

Chapter Seven

Putting Things Off

After Mary-Louisa's death, Francis made a full U-turn, an impressive change of direction in his life. Greatly disappointed by life because of the loss of the person dearest to him, he cut himself off from everything and decided to change course. Or, after walking uncertainly amidst promises and procrastinations, being torn between the attractive things of the world and the appeal of the Gospel's radical demands, he made a clear move in the direction of the consecrated life.

How else can the profound change that appeared in Francis' life around the year 1855 be explained? His family and friends — Henry, Lewis, Teresa, Paul Bonaccia — believed that the decisive factor was his sister's death. On the other hand, those who were intimately familiar with his soul, above all his spiritual director Father Norbert Cassinelli, had no doubt that the death of Mary Louisa was only a step, and not the last one, on a road begun a long time before. The thought of changing directions had been put on hold, but was always present in his life from a time that cannot be precisely identified. Father Norbert himself would say that this change was the result of a tendency that could be traced back to "his earliest years."

When his mother died, Francis was too young to ponder and reflect. But who can say when the gifts of wisdom become part of one's being and how they work? The emptiness in his heart, the prayers before the sculpture of the

Pietà, his father's and sister's explanations about where his mother had gone... Choosing a vocation comes about as the result of making a value judgment on reality, on the relation between this world and the world to come. But the process is begun very early, it starts in one's life experiences before they become a conscious part of one's mental reflections; the process begins before one is even aware of it.

Other experiences in Francis' process of emotional and physical development might very well have given him cause to think about what to do with his life. When, as a little boy, he had been kicked by the pony and saw stars: this episode could have made him stop and think that things might have been worse. Or on hunting trips, when his older brothers would sometimes use the rifle instead of the tree branches covered with birdlime: there was once an accident. In jumping over a ditch, the rifle went off and Francis felt the blast right in his face and heard the buckshot whistle by, fortunately without hitting him. Given to reflective thought as he was, he would not have failed to realize that he could very easily have been killed.

Although the other deaths of family members during his adolescence did not take place in the home, they still very well could have caused him to think about the problem of the final destiny of human beings: Paul died in Chioggia in 1848 and Lawrence killed himself in Rome in 1853.

On his road to religious life, there were at least two episodes where he showed an explicit awareness of being called to it. The first episode probably took place in 1851, when he was thirteen years old. He had fallen ill with a bad throat infection and realized that even the littlest thing could suffice to bring life to an end. This was a very wise reflection on the fragility of human life, while he was undergoing the first phases of adolescence, enjoying life without a care in the world. Lying ill, he promised to become a Religious, perhaps influenced by a desire to imitate his brother Lewis, who had earlier joined the Dominicans and made his religious profession in that same year of 1851. But no sooner had he regained his health and the strength to once more join in on the game of life than his promise slipped into oblivion.

The second resolution to change paths occurred in 1854, probably in the winter. He had fallen ill once more, but this time seriously so; apparently he had contracted acute tonsillitis. With the fever that was consuming him and the tightness in the throat that seemed to suffocate him, he felt that he was about to die, and the unkept promise he had previously made flashed before his mind's eye. Putting everything on the line and insisting with the Lord that he was being sincere, Francis "vowed" to become a Religious if he got well. Since he had been very impressed with the beatification of the Jesuit Andrew Bobola, which had just taken place and had been celebrated with great festivity in the Jesuit school of Spoleto, Francis asked the newly beatified Saint for the grace to get through his illness. That evening, he put the image of the Saint on his throat. The next morning he woke up fully recovered. For the rest of his life he would carry that image with him and would remain always convinced that he had been the recipient of a miracle.

Determined to fulfill his promise, as soon as he started up at school again, he put in a request to join the Jesuits. His request was accepted, but Francis remained at home. Perhaps his father had gotten involved and had told him to wait. Among other things, Francis was indispensable to him at that time as his secretary. It is also possible that there was some hesitation on the part of the Jesuits or that the desire to enjoy life prevailed once more. It appears that Francis himself gave this latter explanation to a close friend later on. In any event, he did not join the Jesuits.

However, Francis had no intention of leaving the matter of religious life entirely behind him. He must have spoken about this question with some of his professors and asked them for advice; one of these was Father Peter Tedeschini. Father Tedeschini was transferred to Rome, but remained in contact with Francis. On May 17, 1855 he answered one of Francis' letters which most certainly dealt with this vocational issue. "The matter at hand has to be handled more with prayer and tears than with any other means." "The world cannot give you the peace that you seek, only Jesus can." Since it was the year of the proclamation of the dogma of the Immaculate Conception of Mary (December 8, 1854) Father Tedeschini advised Francis to ask the Blessed Virgin for enlightenment, suggesting that he make a special novena to her. His ongoing advice soon became a summary of Jesuit spirituality: continuous thoughts of Jesus and Mary, hatred for sin and for the world, flight from bad books and bad friends, contempt for vanity in dress and in conversation, meditation on the eternal truths and frequent reception of the sacraments. In conclusion: "work toward becoming a saint."

He felt the need for guidance and he sought it in every possible place. He had no doubt but that the insistent voice he felt inside was God himself speaking to him, but his father did not want to hear about it — and that too must have been the will of God. There were so many possibilities for the future, how could he be sure which to choose? He even talked about this problem with his Franciscan uncle, Father Fedele da Terni, who was a member of the community of the Franciscan hermitage of Cesi in the province of Terni.

All of this took place before the death of Mary Louisa.

Francis, although fully surrounded by the pleasures of youth and participating in them, was carrying these questions around inside — and they were certainly not easy questions to deal with — when he received the terrible shock of his sister's death.

This umpteenth family tragedy left him even more confused about the significance of the life he was leading and made him feel ever more urgently the need to clarify things and make a decision. The life he had dreamt of and that attracted him so always ended up in disappointment and pain.

As soon as he would let it console him a bit and dazzle him, it would all fall apart and disappear in a puff of smoke. He needed to give himself an answer.

He continued to pray, both with his family and outside the home. At home, he would stop for longer periods of personal prayer before the image of Our Lady of Sorrows. His family noticed that he was regularly placing flowers before the image and "lighting candles and praying there." He was also doing other things, like requesting official records of the studies he had completed with the Jesuits, that made them think that he had some plan in mind.

Noting these changes with some worry, in the autumn of 1855 Sante pressured him more than usual to go to the theater and to various receptions. Francis obeyed, but felt deep inside that he was distancing himself from this world. He would go to the theater, but after a bit would pretend that he had some friend to see or some visit to make and would ask his father's permission to be excused. He would then go off to the Cathedral, which at that period was kept open until late so that the people would have the opportunity to go there and thank Our Lady for rescuing Spoleto from the cholera epidemic, and he would stay there to pray. If he found the Cathedral closed, he would pray in the portico. After his prayer, he would return to his father, usually just as the show was ending, and it would be time to go back home. He would go dancing, but beneath his elegant and tailored suit he probably wore a hair shirt. One day he had not hidden it well in his room and his brother Henry found it and got rid of it. It was made of "rough animal hide with little pieces of sharp metal."

At a certain point, Francis became more explicitly insistent with his father about his vocation as a Religious, but his father explained that he must not be in such a hurry: it would not be good to leave his studies when they were not yet completed; and besides, without Francis' help, Sante would not be able to continue his own work. There would

always be time to take a different path. If after a year he
had not given up this idea of his, Sante promised that he
would give his permission. Francis agreed with the delay,
and in the meantime he got caught up once more with the
magic of youth. Life was beautiful, even if the smile did not
always last long. While it did last, it seemed that nothing
could possibly be better.

Chapter Eight

A Kind of Vocational Thriller

Death always sends shivers down our spine. The same was true for Francis; when someone close to him died or when he himself was frightened by being faced with his own death, he would decide to enter Religious life, but then he would change his mind. This game of deciding one thing and then changing his mind was just too easy. It was simply a sign of immaturity.

It is not ingenuous to admit that death is the most tragic event that we have to experience. Staring at death, we can be filled with hope or with despair. When it is our own death that we face, we are often able to comment on life with deep insight and to make decisions of great significance. When Francis faced death, a certain dissatisfaction with the way he had chosen to live his life came to the surface; this was nothing more than the expression of an internal reality. The origin of this reality cannot be assigned to a precise date, but its presence was a constant feature of Francis' life from 1850 on. Fear of death, however, was not able to separate him from the world of youth in which he lived, the beauty of which he knew how to appreciate and enjoy. Thoughts of death would never succeed in supplanting the intoxicating pleasure of living.

The final phase of his vocational uncertainty was concluded in a period of two weeks, with a combination of events

and coincidences that were as unexpected as they were un-
explainable.

On Friday, August 22, 1856, Francis was participating
in the procession in honor of the Blessed Virgin Mary during the Octave of the Feast of her Assumption, which falls
on August 15. The venerated icon of Our Lady from the Cathedral was paraded through the streets. The residents of
Spoleto were particularly devoted to Our Lady and attrib-
uted to her numerous interventions on behalf of the city,
protecting it throughout its history. Francis was more or less
distracted as he participated in the celebration, being moti-
vated more by curiosity than by devotion. But he did not
want to miss being a part of this public display of veneration, for he always felt a particular affinity for pious devotion to Mary. But it was perhaps the first time that he took
part in such a procession with very little internal involve-
ment.

As the image passed him, he had the feeling that Our
Lady was looking directly at him, staring right into his eyes
— this is the effect that Eastern icons have — and he could
hear a voice speaking very clearly within him: Francis, do
you not understand that this life is not for you? Become a
Religious. What are you waiting for?

This was an interior experience of the supernatural order, one that is difficult to analyze, but the effects were such
that from that moment on Francis was completely changed.
His benumbed will and dissipated psychological strength
started to function with full awareness again. He felt that
"his heart had been changed." His whole life finally clicked
into place. After that event, he saw with single-minded clarity the road that lay before him, and no one would be able to
stop him: not father or brothers; neither friends nor priests.
He was so determined in his decision that he no longer looked
at the past or at the obstacles that were still present, but
looked only to the future. It only took one person to make
Francis give in: Our Lady.

The first person to receive this young man, now in flight from the world and on his way to new destinations, was the Jesuit priest Father Charles Bompiani, his teacher and perhaps confessor. On Sunday, August 24, Francis asked to talk to him. They met after lunch and talked in the philosophy classroom. Francis told him about the episode with the icon and explained to him the determination that he felt inside. Mysteriously enough, the choice of the Passionists had already been made, without the slightest discussion. So great was the persuasive power expressed and radiated by Francis that Father Bompiani, as a Jesuit well trained in discernment, had no doubt that this was a genuine call from God. He reassured Francis and encouraged him in his choice, making him understand that his father's permission was indispensable. In the meantime, the request for admission to the Passionists had already been sent to Recanati (in the province of Macerata), where the Provincial Superior had his residence.

Even Sante realized that the Francis now standing before him was no longer the Francis of before. He was dumbstruck when he heard that Francis had decided on the Passionists. He could accept the Jesuits, about whom they had spoken earlier; they were an Order with cultural prestige and a way of life that was more tolerable. But did Francis realize who the Passionists were? How would he ever last, very particular as he was, in such a penitential lifestyle? But Francis had already considered all that, and explained that there was nothing to worry about. The request for admission was already on its way to its destination. The year set aside for thinking about a religious vocation had passed, and now the promise had to be kept. This was the right moment and he did not intend to wait any longer.

Sante was at a loss; he felt trapped, realizing that this time there was no way out. This was no longer the Francis easily swayed, who liked to consider the various possibilities, who would sweet-talk everyone to get his way and who would run off scared if you so much as made a face at him. He now had the determination of steel. The talk ended before it reached a conclusion. They would finish it later, maybe the following day. In the meantime, Lewis, the Dominican, was at home; he had come from Livorno to spend some vacation time with the family. Sante asked him to talk to his brother and to get out of his head at least the strange desire to shut himself up with the Passionists. At the same time, a letter arrived from Recanati for Francis; it granted his request to join the Passionists: he was instructed to go to Morrovalle as soon as possible. But Sante hid the letter and said nothing to Francis about it. Lewis' attempts to dissuade him were also an utter failure. On the contrary, since Francis had not yet received a response from the Passionist Provincial, he sent off another letter, asking once more to be admitted.

Finally, Sante was honest with himself and realized that he had been overreacting in trying to keep Francis under control. He had recourse to his faith and made the effort to see the "adorable will of God" in all this. He told Francis that, as his father, he would give him his blessing: he could make preparations for his departure, the answer of the Passionist Provincial had already arrived. They both agreed on the 6th of September as his departure date, since there was a school assembly at which Francis would recite on September 5th. He had been preparing this recitation with his friends for some time; it was to mark the close of the academic year and the beginning of fall vacation, which would last until November 5th.

With the situation now resolved, Francis' first desire was to thank Our Lady. He did so first in the privacy of his own heart, praying before the home shrine where the sculpture of the Pietà was located. He then went to the Church of Saint Luke in Spoleto, where he prayed before the image of Our Lady of Sorrows, savoring the gift that was his in now having this certainty.

Another unusual occurrence in the unfolding of these final events was the uncommon promptness with which the Passionist Provincial accepted Francis' request for admission. The usual course of action required that, before acceptance, a candidate come to the Passionist House in person, so that those responsible for formation could make an initial evaluation and so that information on the candidate's prior life could be gathered. In Francis' case, however, the Provincial responded by return mail, granting him admission without placing any conditions, except for the formality of a record of the studies he had completed and the payment of 28 scudi, about 30 dollars, to cover the cost of two habits and a cloak. What did Francis say in his two letters to convince the Provincial that "his decision to become a Religious was not the result of the irresponsible enthusiasm of youth but the result of a true and legitimate vocation"?

The reason he chose the Passionists is not known. In the Possenti household the Passionists must have been known, given Sante's reaction, but we do not know how. Perhaps they passed through Spoleto from their nearby Religious House in Todi on one of their fund-raising tours, or maybe Pacifica's husband, also from Todi, spoke of them. It is possible that they were known in the area around Spoleto for the missions they would preach or because of the time they came to Spoleto from Morrovalle to buy blankets for fifty scudi. Maybe they were remembered from when they attempted to found a Religious House in Spoleto or in Trevi, or from when they were invited to preach to the Sodality of Mary. Perhaps Francis was impressed by the beatification of Saint Paul of the Cross, the founder of the Passionists, which took place on May 1, 1853, raising much interest in Francis' Spoleto school and in the magazine "*La Civiltà Cattolica*," which began publication in that same period. To prepare for the celebrations, two Passionist Brothers had come to Spoleto asking for contributions. Francis would have most certainly spoke about this project with his classmates

Caesar Calandrelli and Ponziano Gismondi, both of whom left for the Passionist novitiate in Morrovalle on September 3rd, three days before Francis.

The beginning of that September, Francis got the last of the school records that he needed for the novitiate, he paid his instructor Philip Fabi for some books that he had received earlier and he mentally prepared himself for the school assembly in honor of Mary. This was the school assembly program that he had been preparing with his friends, which would take place the evening of September 5th in the Church of the Immaculate Conception, also known as Our Lady of Piaggia. This church was part of the Jesuit school building. That same evening, the students would also receive their scholastic awards.

At the assembly, Francis gave the most splendid performance of his career. He put on the best clothes he had and also wore the best of whatever he could find at home. He was dressed in "the finest suit" with the accompaniment of some "worldly trinkets" of Michael's; he wanted to make a sensational impression. His friend Paul Bonaccia, who was present, described him in terms that are almost seductive: "more handsome than usual," with elegant clothes, every strand of hair meticulously in place, white gloves, shining shoes, a form-fitting vest, a dazzlingly white pleated shirt with a sparkling gem and stud at his chest, bright buttons, starched cuffs and collar, a silk tie; everything reflecting the latest taste of the times, and the dreamy face of one who is in ecstasy at the feast of life, wearing "in triumph the most recent styles." He was truly a splendor to behold.

The school assembly was dedicated to Our Lady of Piaggia, another venerated image of Mary in Spoleto, and Francis made three different presentations: the introductory speech, a brief historical summary, and the recitation of the ballad of Our Lady of Piaggia, all written by him. He was a great success, receiving long applause and comments full of admiration; to say nothing of the swooning sighs of the girls, especially Mary Pennacchietti who was devouring him with her eyes. The apostolic delegate, who was present along with the Bishop and other local authorities, gave full expression to his own enthusiasm and told Sante that he wanted to give a hug to that jewel of a son. For a moment Sante indulged in some self-delusion, pretending that Francis' departure planned for the following day was only a bad dream.

But this was Francis' final act. He had wanted to settle completely his debt to the world that he had loved and that had taken him in, making room for him and offering him the real possibility of fulfilling himself. Having now done this, it was time to move on. With the curtain having gone down and silence once again reigning, he bid a few close friends good-bye, talking vaguely about a trip, but leaving open the question of his return. To Mary Pennacchietti he whispered, "We'll see each other tomorrow." A lie, but perhaps justified in that whatever pain she might feel would be put off till later. Then he stayed out till very late with his friend Parenzio Parenzi; "it seemed like he could not bring himself to say good-bye." But he did not have the courage to tell him everything. The next day Parenzio would receive a letter in which Francis explained his decision to leave, asking for prayers.

Spoleto the day after: the news traveled through the city like wildfire. The assessor's son had disappeared; had he been kidnapped? No, he had joined the Passionists! Unbelievable!

Later, when the school year reopened, the Jesuit professor Father Lewis Pincelli began the rhetoric lesson with the question: "Have you heard about the dancer? Who would have thought!"

Francis was gone, he had removed himself from the world where he had been a big hit. He was eighteen years, six months and six days old. He could be considered mature if maturity was the ability to make a decision and accept responsibility for oneself. For him, maturity had arrived simultaneously with his definitive decision. He could have decided to get married, but instead he decided to go away.

Chapter Nine

No Use Trying to Sabotage the Road

Everything could still go up in smoke. Not so much because of the further questioning that Sante made him undergo during the long trip to Morrovalle, but because of something even more enigmatic that his father had lovingly concocted for him.

Francis would one day confide that his immediate acceptance by the Passionist Provincial was providential. If his departure had been put back even one day, his decision to become a Religious would have disappeared once more, but this time for good. The very evening of September 6th, "such a terrible danger was awaiting him that he would have once more sought refuge in the world, he would have spoiled God's plan, and might have even lost his eternal salvation." On December 31, 1857, he would write to his brother Michael: "If I had waited one moment longer, perhaps I would not be where I am now."

The situation was most likely this: Sante had decided, with his mind's rigorous logic, that it was not reasonable to put himself in the way of Francis' vocation once again. Therefore, he agreed that Francis could leave on September 6th. But in the logic of his heart, which is quite another thing, he could not accept being separated from this son also; Francis was dearer to him than all the others. Since he had the impression in the last few months that Francis' interest in the Pennacchietti girl had grown, and that she herself would certainly go along most willingly with this plan, he consulted with the family and they agreed to have a party the evening of that very day, September 6th, when Francis was supposed to leave. Who knows, wondered Sante, if between the warmth of their beating hearts and the rhythms of the dance, Francis and Mary Pennacchietti would not end up becoming engaged?

But it was all an illusion. Francis understood everything, but pretended to know nothing about it. They would just have to have the party without him! He finished up his duties at the school assembly and the morning of the 6th he left. Sante placed his final hopes in two letters that he addressed to two priests who were relatives on his wife's side of the family; one was to be given to Canon Caesar Acquacotta, Pro-Vicar General for Loreto, and the other to Father John Baptist Frisciotti, superior of the Capuchin monastery in Morrovalle. He charged the two priests to question Francis and see if he was really serious; and, if possible, they were to get him to reconsider his decision.

The departure from Spoleto took place while the city was still asleep. He gave hugs to his father, his brothers and Pacifica. It was useless trying to hide the tears. What emptiness was now felt in the big Possenti house! There remained only Vincent, who had assumed the role of Sante's new secretary, and Henry, who was going to the seminary.

Francis' official companion for the trip was his brother, the Dominican priest Father Lewis, who was on his way back to Livorno but wanted to make a stop at Loreto. Francis was pleased to stop in Loreto too, as he would thus be able to fulfill an old dream, to pray in Our Lady's house.

Travelling in the coach there was also a priest from Spoleto, and two children from Rome with their governess. Francis and Lewis were seated in the exposed front of the coach with the driver, the other passengers were inside. The changing scenery, valleys, hills and mountains, first of Umbria then of the Marches, made the trip pleasant. It was also made pleasant by the joy of his new life, which now outweighed the sadness of leaving home. At 11:00 p.m. they stopped for the night, perhaps at Matelica where Francis had relatives on his mother's side.

The next day, after only a few hours of travelling, they could see Loreto in the distance, but their arrival in the city was delayed by a "terrible thunderstorm." They arrived in Loreto late in the day while it was still pouring rain, and they learned that there was no room in any of the hotels because of the upcoming feast of Our Lady of Loreto. The Basilica was already closed and they had to make due with praying outside from afar. They were able to camp out in the reception hall of a hotel "at the beginning of the Square where the Holy House is"; emergency straw mattresses were brought out for sleeping. The rain had flooded the Square where a large crowd of pilgrims from Ciociaria, who were unsuccessful at finding lodging even under the colonnade, were soaking wet and singing to Our Lady.

When the rain finally stopped, it was already night. Francis and Lewis stepped out to say hello to Canon Acquacotta, who was staying with the Sisters of the Visitation in the Montereale section of town, and to give him the letter from Sante. They were invited to lunch for the following day.

September 8th, feast of the Nativity of Our Lady, is a great holiday in Loreto. Francis spent the morning in the Holy House, not leaving it even for the solemn Pontifical Mass going on in the Basilica. A prolonged prayer, cut off from everything and immersed in the world of God. He made a general confession to bring to an end a part of his life that did not exist any longer. Then he received Communion, where he experienced Christ with a newfound intimacy, free from every encumbrance.

Then lunch at his uncle's, the Canon. He listened a little absent-mindedly to the grim picture which his uncle painted of the Passionists' life. His uncle was well acquainted with their life, having taken refuge with them during the turmoil of 1848. Francis respectfully informed his uncle that he had considered all that; everything had already been carefully thought out, and he had no doubts about the choice he had made. He waited for the prelate to conclude his awkward attempt at getting him to change his mind, and then he went off to pray at the Holy House of Our Lady, where he spent the rest of the afternoon. This stop at Loreto, seen by others as the first of two final tests to get him to change his mind, was for him a tremendous grace that brought to its climax the grace of two weeks earlier at Spoleto, and which was the prelude of many more graces to follow.

He left the Basilica only when it was closing time, and tried to bring a souvenir with him, prying a piece of plaster from the wall of the Holy House. Meanwhile, the Canon sent his observations off to Sante: the boy was unyielding; Sante would have to let him go. The day, filled with people, sights and emotion, had also included a short visit with some Jesuit friends at the Illyrian College.

The morning of the 9th there was again prayer and communion at Loreto, and then an eight o'clock departure for Morrovalle, passing through Civitanova. They made only a brief stop there to greet some relatives of his mother, but he had to put up with some jokes and stupid statements from people who pretended to be astounded at the reason for the trip. These comments, which were just empty words, annoyed him only briefly. In any event, they were soon off and on their way to Morrovalle.

At lunchtime, they were with the Capuchins where his uncle Father John Baptist Frisciotti from Civitanova was the superior and welcomed them. And once more, under instructions from Sante, Francis was put to the test, the final one. Again, a commentary on the life of the Passionists was made, with the difficulties overstated and exaggerated. Have you ever heard how coarse the Capuchin habits are? The Passionist habits are "a thousand times twice as rough!" A waste of breath. Francis reacted like a champion hurdler who, with muscles all ready at the beginning of the race and himself filled with the desire to win, was not even aware of the hurdles. Sante would soon receive a second report, from the second and final attempt to sabotage the road: he cannot be stopped.

A short distance more and they arrived at the Passionist House, just west of Morrovalle. They had intended to make only a brief stop for introductions and to drop off the baggage, because the next day they had planned to go, together with his Capuchin uncle, on a trip to Montegiorgio to visit an aunt who was a nun, Sister Mary Teresa Frisciotti, in the Convent of Saint Augustine. But Francis, once he had set foot in the House, no longer wanted to hear talk of leaving; he bid good-bye to everyone, making them understand that he would not leave for anyone or anything. The Passionists of Morrovalle welcomed him with such warmth and love that the Dominican Father Lewis was moved to tears. He was alone when he left the Passionist House and spent the night with the Capuchins. The next day he stopped in at the Passionist House once more to make sure that there were no second thoughts or desires to return home. Francis was very happy there and he asked his uncle to let his father know.

A few days afterward, Francis himself would write to Sante, beginning his letter with a solemn tone used in important proclamations: "God the Almighty had been waiting for me for a very long time, and I, like an ingrate, acted like I did not hear." Now "the day has come." He would begin the novitiate and take the Passionist habit. Of the old Francis, the Francis of before, there would no longer remain anything; not even the name.

The Passionist

Chapter Ten

Making Himself at Home

It seemed as though he were born there. When he arrived the other day it was as if he were going more to a ballroom than to a Religious House, but now he could no longer be distinguished from the others. His curly locks and the rest of his hair was shorn, and it was a pity to see him with a shaven head. His desire to be always in the spotlight was left behind in Spoleto. He was no longer a heart-throb because he was now the one with the subdued heart, wanting to lose himself in the love that he had discovered.

The choice that he had made was decisive not only because it freed him from anxiety, but because it gave him true resolve. He no longer had to go around in search of something, because he had found what he was looking for.

Once a candidate for the Passionists has entered the novitiate, he usually undergoes a period of observation, but Francis was dispensed from this formality. Since the day after his arrival there was a group about to go on spiritual retreat in preparation for taking the habit, Francis was quickly made a part of that group.

Sunday morning, September 21, he received the Passionist habit from the novice master, Father Raphael Ricci.

As a sign that all was now new and that the past no longer existed, he dropped the name Francis and took that of Gabriel. Since the Passionists also had the custom of re-

65

placing the family name with some Christian mystery to which the individual wanted to be joined and with which he wanted to be identified, Gabriel chose the title "Our Lady of Sorrows." Gabriel of Mary Our Lady of Sorrows was his new name.

While he was being vested in the Passionist habit, signifying that he was now one of them, he was so moved that he cried. It was clear that he was really doing it. He seemed to have been made for this kind of life, and it seemed to have been made for him. "It seems that he has been a Religious for a long time." His two former classmates from Spoleto were very surprised; he was not one who committed himself only half-way.

He felt he should send a note to his father right away; poor Sante, left behind in Spoleto with an empty space not only in the house but also in his heart. Gabriel put pen to paper and wrote: "I cannot tell you how much joy was mine when I put on the Religious habit; I have taken the name Gabriel of Our Lady of Sorrows. The happiness and joy that I feel in this house cannot be described; the pleasures I had in the outside world cannot be compared to them. I would not trade even fifteen minutes of being here inside, praying before Our Lady, with a year or any amount of time filled with shows and other pastimes of Spoleto. Indeed, my life is filled with happiness."

In what did all this rapture consist? This was his schedule: at night, five hours of sleep, one and a half hours of prayer, and then two or three hours more of sleep; in the morning, prayer, two Masses, breakfast, studying, work and instruction, a walk in the orchard, midday prayer, and then lunch. After lunch there was time for talking with his fellow novices, an hour siesta, vespers and reading of spiritual books, a procession through the corridors of the Passionist House with the image of Our Lady, more studying, work and a relaxing stroll, an hour of meditation and then supper. The day would end with some restful time in community, praying the rosary and bedding down for the night. He wrote that twenty-four hours flew by like many "brief instants."

The novices were separate from the other members of the community, although they lived with the other Religious who would come and go, being involved in different pastoral activities and having other duties. There were nine novices: two from Rome, three from Spoleto, one from Perugia and three from the Kingdom of the two Sicilies. The novice master Father Raphael Ricci was responsible for guiding their spiritual growth and instructing them on the requirements of this new life; he was a holy man and experienced in the formation of novices. His assistant was Father Norbert Cassinelli, who, younger than Father Ricci, was only nine years older than Gabriel; he too had entered Religious life after hearing a voice during a procession in honor of Our Lady.

The Passionist family at this time was experiencing a good moment in their history. It was a period of activity and vitality with new houses being founded abroad and ambitious plans for the future. The Passionists were engaged in work in the mission lands, they were involved with ecumenism and above all with the renewal of the local churches where they would preach missions that stirred people's consciences and prompted them to make changes in their lives.

The Province to which Gabriel belonged had been established five years earlier, in 1851. It included the central regions of Emilia and Romagna, the Marches, Umbria and Abruzzi. It was called the Province of Our Most Blessed Lady of the Pietà and was a Province that was zealous in its commitment to holiness, a commitment inherited from the tradition of the Institute, founded by Saint Paul of the Cross in 1720. This commitment was so demanding that many aspirants were not able to live up to it. In fact, the very year that Gabriel was in the novitiate, seven young priests between the ages of twenty-two and twenty-eight left the Province.

Morrovalle, where the novitiate was located, was the center of all this spiritual dynamism. The lessons given by Raphael and Norbert, whose duty it was to see to the spiritual formation of the new arrivals, focused on the Passion of Christ, as the charism of the Passionists required, and they also placed great emphasis on the role of the Blessed Virgin Mary in the interior lives of the youth. So great was this emphasis that it gave rise to a movement known as the Marian School of Morrovalle.

The Passionist community was seen by the people as a special presence and sign. The country folk of the surrounding area arranged their day according to the rhythm established by the bells of the Passionist House as they rang out to mark the different times of prayer. The bells served as the countryside's wake-up call, as the call to lunch and supper, and the summer night-time call to go into the fields for the harvest. The townspeople would always find the doors of the Passionist House open and they could go there freely to ask for advice or to receive the sacraments. The poor could make use of the "snack room" where they could have something to eat and hear some encouraging words. A short while before Gabriel arrived, the cholera epidemic had swept through Morrovalle, but the Passionists had not left and none of them were stricken.

Gabriel immediately fell in love with his new family. He liked everything: the House, the Rules, the way of life, the daily rhythms, the bell that called them to prayer and to meetings, the delight of praising God in the middle of the night while the townspeople slept and of praying silently for hours and hours with the shutters closed, the silence during the day, walking with his eyes lowered, the habit, the sandals with bare feet inside. He said that he would not trade the habit even for a king's royal robes. He once confided to a fellow novice that he had seen so many places and experienced so many pleasures and delights, but none like those he experienced in the Passionist House.

Of course there were also difficulties, but he faced them with the courage of a lion. Were something to happen that might separate him from his Passionist family, "I would come back at once" — he wrote — "and embrace this life again, re-establishing the ties that bind me to it." And another time, "If I had to choose a Congregation all over again, I would take this one a thousand times over!" Even if the Religious Houses were closed, as had been threatened in the past, "I would never go back home."

The steady rhythm of this life, in which provisions were made for everything and every moment was filled with something for him to do, gave him the certainty that he had truly found God's will and every worry was removed from his mind. Thus he could remain enfolded by God's loving presence without being distracted. In fact, he wanted nothing else. He did not even want to read the letters that his father often sent enquiring about how he was. It was sufficient that the novice master tell him if there were some important news. There was never a word spoken about his family or about his former life in Spoleto, except words of regret for the time wasted, or words recounting how much better things were now than in the past. He wanted to speak only of the Crucified Lord, of Our Lady, of his great fortune in finding this present life, of the enchantment brought on by being full of this love.

His father was insistent in wanting to visit him, using the pretext that he was going to Montegiorgio to see Sister Mary Teresa Frisciotti, Francis' aunt. But like a good diplomat, Gabriel managed to say and do what was necessary to have the visit put off and then to have it canceled altogether. He explained to his father that while he was in the novitiate he did not want any distractions; after he had completed the novitiate he said that the Passionists were not accustomed to such visits.

In May of 1857, Pope Pius IX made a visit to the Papal States to improve relations with his subjects after the turmoil of the years 1848 - 1850. He passed through the nearby city of Civitanova on his way to Fermo from Loreto and then again upon returning to Loreto from Fermo. Gabriel and his fellow novices did not go to see the Pope, preferring to be close to him with their acts of mortification and their prayers for him.

Since Gabriel came from an aristocratic background, and because his father was elderly and a widower, the Superiors did not want him cut off from his family. They therefore had Gabriel write to Sante at least once a month. Gabriel accepted this as an act of mortification, but took advantage of the situation to give advice to his brothers, to repeat how happy he was, to tell how sorry he was for the stupid things he used to do at home, and to put their minds at ease about his state of health — in fact he had put on a few pounds and had never felt better in his life. He thrived on the penitential practices of the Passionists. He would fast and abstain from meat three times a week, and not just during Advent and Lent. But there was always an abundance of fruit and dairy products. In the mornings there was no coffee with milk, but the toast with diluted wine, according to the custom of the monks of Saint Silvester in the Marches. In any event, to listen to him, he could not have been better.

Who would have recognized him? How can it be explained? Quite simply, he had found deeper values and felt fulfilled. Not that what he had first were not values; friendships, making a good impression, trips out into the country, being stylish, success in school, showing off with friends: these can all be good things and can sometimes be important, but they are transitory, based on things that do not last. Francis needed to find deeper meaning in life. While he was dedicated to those fading values, although he would give his all to enjoy them, he never felt completely satisfied. The movement from superficial values to deeper ones came with the choices he made when he matured. Love with a woman could be an excellent vocation, all the more so since that was the direction he had headed off in. But the Lord had called him elsewhere.

Tuesday, September 22, 1857, Gabriel finished the novitiate and became a Passionist by making his Religious profession, that is, he committed himself publicly before God and the Church to practice poverty, chastity and obedience, and to promote devotion to the Crucified Lord. The novice master Father Raphael presided at the celebration. Of Francis' two former classmates from Spoleto, Caesar Calandrelli left because of uncertainties about his health and about his vocation; the other one, Ponziano Gismondi, made his profession and took the name of Ermenegildo, but later he too left.

A few days after his profession, he wrote to his father: "By the grace of God and the protection of the Blessed Virgin Mary, Our Lady of Sorrows, to my own indescribable joy and consolation, my desires have been satisfied and I have made my holy profession. It is such a great grace that it cannot be put into words."

Everything was so overwhelming that words were not adequate to recount it all: the joy, the consolation, the grace received.

Poverty, chastity, obedience; the Crucified Lord, Our Lady of Sorrows; virtue, the salvation of others. These were the new challenges where he would once again triumph and come in first, the new stage on which he would shine.

Chapter Eleven

A Whole Lifetime of School

Countrysides neatly arranged as gardens: the hills and valleys were covered with a soft green which in the summer turned to shades of gold as the harvest approached. From Pievetorina, Tolentino, Recanati and Loreto the contours of the land rose and fell, seeming to create waves that were reflected from Macerata, Montelupone, Morrovalle, Fermo, Montegranaro, Montegiorgio and Upper Civitanova, and that plumbed the depths of the Esino, Musone, Potenza and Chienti River Valleys. This was the lay of the land in the Marches where Gabriel spent the first three years of his Passionist life, from September of 1856 to July of 1859.

After completing the novitiate, he remained in Morrovalle for nine months, waiting for other novices to finish their year of probation; in this way, he would be part of a small group that would be sent to another community where together they would all begin studies in preparation for priesthood. He did not lose any time. Now that he had learned how to put God at the very center of his life and how to be always with him, he needed to get used to academic studies again. He had been away from textbooks for a year, because he needed to accustom himself to a new way of thinking, feeling and living. But now that this was all clear, school once again came to be a part of his life, and it would be a dominant part until the end. For the rest of his days he would remain a student. But studying was somehow very different now that it had a clear and appealing purpose: priest-hood and the life of a missionary. It would become an insepa-rable part of his interior experience; it would help him to give himself more completely to God and would be an extension of his prayer. But it would still be school: he would have to go to class, learn the lessons and prepare for exams.

He could have proceeded directly to the study of theol-ogy since he had already taken courses in humanities and philosophy in Spoleto at the prestigious Jesuit school. But his Passionist Superiors had him repeat a year so that he could review his Latin and so that they could evaluate bet-ter the background in philosophy that he had received in Spoleto, for it was essential to have a solid grounding in Thomistic philosophy. Gabriel wrote to his father that his "present studies revolve around Latin" and, later, that he had "begun once again to study philosophy."

His intellectual formation was demanding. It was nec-essary to have a strong grasp of logic and metaphysics, and to have a good understanding of the Bible and know how to make use of the Sacred Scriptures. The theological frame-work was a little bit out of touch with the historical reali-ties of the time, as was true everywhere in that period. Can-didates to the priesthood were taught how to refute the er-rors of the past but not how to confront the errors that in the present were spreading through society, such as commu-nism, which was an outgrowth of rationalism and secular-ism.

The textbooks used were the traditional Thomistic col-lections, which based arguments on the Bible, the Church's magisterial teachings, tradition and reason. This was a solid and thorough preparation. The only real disadvantage was that when these young men finished their studies, they would find that the social situation had changed. It was true that a new scholastic method had been prepared by the Passionist Dominic Barberi, today among those officially declared "Blessed" by the Church, but this new method was never published because the Superiors believed it to be innovative, and the policy of the day was "things new are always to be shunned." And there was at that time no questioning of that policy.

To develop their spiritual formation, Passionist students followed more or less the same daily schedules that they had followed as novices, with the only real difference being that instead of studying the history and way of life of the Passionist family, they studied scholastic disciplines. The amount of time set aside for prayer and the personal diligence required was just about the same. There were frequent meetings with those responsible for evaluating the students' spiritual growth. Their educational training became more focused; there was not a broad and diverse spectrum of material presented, instead there were just a handful of topics that were examined in depth. The students discussed such subjects as interior unity in conformity to the Crucified Lord, rule and authority as an objective manifestation of God's will, and devotion to Our Lady. They were also encouraged to develop as many pious practices as they could.

The main focus of all this was the Crucified Lord, for on this depended everything else, such as the proper means to choose in order to perfect oneself and to attain true apostolic commitment. "In Christ's Passion there is everything": this phrase was the founder's mark of genius and permeated all aspects of the Passionist family as the essential spiritual kernel that every member had to make his own.

Those Religious who seriously accepted this challenge achieved a firm, unshakable virtue that could stand up to anything. Those who did not accept it seriously ended up merely putting on an act and either remained in the community barely getting by, or they simply left, choosing a different path. Many young men who joined the Passionists had the same interior fortitude as Gabriel, though not all of them would be officially recognized by the Church as Saints.

September 22, 1857 not only meant the end of the novitiate for Gabriel and the beginning of his formal studies, but it also brought another very important change: having finished the novitiate, Gabriel's formational relationship with Father Raphael Ricci ended and he would now be under the guidance of Father Norbert Cassinelli, who up till then had been assistant novice master. Father Norbert had been named director of the students and was also to be their professor. He would remain responsible for Gabriel's spiritual and intellectual formation until the end. No one would know Gabriel as well as he did. They would meet every two weeks to appraise and make adjustments in his interior life. He would be the principal mediator of the work God wrought in Gabriel; he was both an amazed observer and a capable director in the wonderful as well as in the difficult moments of Gabriel's growth. He would also be the one to whom Gabriel would normally go to confession. Over and over again, with humble pride, he would repeat that Gabriel never hid anything from him, that it was a delight to move about freely in his unencumbered soul, that "it was beautiful giving him spiritual guidance," that Gabriel inspired in Norbert's own soul "a sense of veneration," that he could not think of him without becoming very emotional. "From that moment on we were no longer separable; only death came between us."

After the novitiate, the interlude at Morrovalle served to help Gabriel test the strength of his desire to embrace the Passionist ideals. There was no difference from when he was a novice. He made the same concerted effort to see that no distracting elements entered into his life. He good-naturedly put up with the pestering intrusions of his Capuchin uncle, who, from his nearby monastery, acted as Sante's special delegate for everything, always bringing news and asking for news to send back, as if there could never be enough.

In April of 1858 he had to go before a notary public in Fermo to take care of some official family business; his sister Teresa, who had in the meantime moved with her husband to the Marches, was also there. Norbert accompanied him on this trip, as the Passionist rules required. In the presence of his sister he was very composed and kept his eyes lowered without saying anything until his director told him that he really should make some conversation. Seeing him acting that way, Teresa felt a pain in her heart; according to her he was not well.

During the trip, Gabriel and Norbert made a stop-over with the Jesuits of Fermo. The Rector there was Father Rossi, who knew Gabriel, now a Passionist student, when he was a student in the Jesuit school of Spoleto. Calling Norbert aside, he asked him: "How is it going with this boy? He was not too serious." "His vocation has made him a different person," Norbert reassured him. "If he goes on like he's doing now, there's no doubt about his becoming a true saint."

During the same period, on April 26th, there arrived the sad news that the twenty-three-year-old Passionist student Peter Porfiri, a native of Morrovalle, had died of tuberculosis in the Passionist House of Isola del Gran Sasso. Gabriel understood the pain of the family members who came to the House in order to get more precise information about the death and to be consoled. But deep inside he thought that Peter had really been fortunate to return to God at such an early age. And Gabriel, always quick to act and ever eager to make his desires become reality, asked for the grace to die young himself, and to die of tuberculosis no less, because with tuberculosis the mind remained lucid and one could still perform acts of love right up to the very end.

Although he may have acted in a moment of impetuosity, he was not insincere. Therefore Gabriel confided to his spiritual director that he was praying for this favor. "May it never be so!" was Norbert's reaction, fearful that the Eternal Father might actually grant Gabriel's request. The most one could do, Norbert explained, was to ask for such a grace "if it brought glory to God and if it were for the good of the soul." Precisely the proper conditions. The death of the young student of Isola del Gran Sasso was a general rehearsal for what would happen less than four years later.

Finally it was decided that, for the academic year 1858 - 1859, the group of students who had been prepared during the last few months of the novitiate should be transferred to Pievetorina, still in the province of Macerata, near the Apennine mountains of the Marches. Before leaving, Gabriel received permission to say good-bye to his uncle who was the superior of the Capuchins. Another student, Atanasio Morganti, went with him. His uncle, Father John Baptist, seemed to have finally understood that this was Francis' vocation and did not dare to question his nephew this time about his choice to become a Passionist.

On June 20, 1858, the group left Morrovalle under the direction of Father Norbert and headed for their new destination, possibly going straight up the Chienti Valley, passing through Macerata and Tolentino. They remained there one year and fifteen days, completing their philosophy studies and beginning their formal theological training.

During the stay in Pievetorina, there were some surprises for Gabriel. The first one was a bad throat infection. There it was again, the usual inflammation that made his throat very tight and sore; but Gabriel was already familiar with it and it no longer frightened him as much as it used to. Finally, it cleared up, but who knows if it was only the throat.

The second surprise was a visit from Pacifica Cucchi, the Possenti's family helper in Spoleto. She had not sought anyone's advice on making this visit, nor had she sought permission, but just showed up one bright August day, overjoyed and affectionate as a mother would have been. She was very curious to see him and recommended that he eat well. But she found it difficult to understand the new Francis.

In September, Michael also came — at the time he was studying medicine in Rome — and stayed with his brother for two days. He had not seen him for a couple of years and he thought he looked weak. He tried asking him, "Why don't you come back home?" "I'm happy here and I have everything I need. The Lord has given me a tremendous grace that I had never imagined would be mine." Michael had brought him a golden heart-shaped locket, like those that fiancés give each other, and suggested that he could put something inside, like a relic. Was he kidding, Gabriel must have thought; and Michael realized that "he was almost offended," for the Passionists are not allowed to own personal possessions.

Michael was not able to get Gabriel to promise to write more often, but he did at least get a promise that he would be notified if there were any serious health problems. Gabriel's director also guaranteed this.

The two of them got along very well during the two days that they spent together. Gabriel realized that Michael was not called to religious life, as he had thought earlier; but he could be a very good layman. For this reason, Gabriel gave him all kinds of useful advice. While they were walking through the garden and talking, the flower bed that Gabriel was tending for Our Lady caught Michael's eye and he could not stop admiring it. It was an explosion of daisies. Gabriel felt that Michael would like to have one of the flowers and instinctively picked one, offering it to him. Then, coming upon his director, he knelt before him and asked pardon for having done this without asking permission: for a Passionist did not own anything as his own.

Michael left Pievetorina apprehensive about his brother's health. His eyes were already being trained to look at things as a doctor, and there was something that made him suspicious about Gabriel's health. He would remember the affectionate good-bye kiss from Gabriel, "on the left cheek."

Winter in the mountains was bitter, but the young men withstood it well. In the classroom, they gathered around the stove and in their enthusiasm they did not think of the cold as a problem.

Spring, even if it came late, brought refreshment to their lungs, filling them with crisp air. Most of the time, they were busy with books or in chapel, but every once in a while they would go for walks among the narrow cliff-edged valleys and brooks of the Apennines. The town of Visso was not far, and the students would sometimes make a pleasant outing to the little Shrine of Our Lady of Macereto, with Norbert gladly accompanying them.

A small group of boys who come to the Passionist House for private lessons noticed that after lunch Gabriel would go off by himself and disappear among the trees of the woods. One time they spread out in the woods to see what he was up to and they spied him gathering stones from the Chienti River, which at that point was little more than a stream; he would kneel on these stones and pray before an image of Our Lady. Local tradition has preserved this fact and, turning it into a legend, sees Gabriel in ecstasy, lifted from the earth with his arms opened wide.

The Superiors' plan was that Gabriel's group would remain in Pievetorina until 1860, after which they would be transferred to Recanati when the Passionist House there would have room to accommodate them. But before the established time, it became necessary to take in also the young men from the retreat house in Todi; unfortunately, because of the level of studies which the Todi group was at, they could not be assimilated into any already existing group. As a solution to this problem, therefore, it was decided to send the Pievetorina students to Isola del Gran Sasso and those from Todi to Pievetorina. Accordingly, on July 4, 1859, Norbert and his squad of seven students set out for Isola del Gran Sasso in Abruzzi, in the Kingdom of Naples.

It was still planned that Gabriel's group would be transferred to Recanati in 1860, only now they would be moved from Isola del Gran Sasso instead of from Pievetorina. But the uncertain political situation and the threat of a Piedmontese invasion put that plan on hold. The

Piedmontese did in fact descend upon the land in September and the Passionist House at Recanati was made into a hospital for those wounded in the Battle of Castelfidardo. After the hostilities, when the House was finally left empty, it was thought that the Isola students could finally go there; but on January 3, 1861, the law suppressing Religious Orders was put into effect in the Marches. However, it was not strictly enforced and Religious Congregations were allowed to continue. Thus at the end of the year, when it was no longer permitted that Holy Orders be conferred on anyone in the ex-Kingdom of Naples, the Superiors decided that the group of Isola del Gran Sasso should return to the Marches. In July of 1862 they returned, settling in Recanati, but Gabriel had already left this world.

His group had left Pievetorina early on the morning of July 4th, and they made it to Recanati in one day; they had a good little carriage and the road was downhill or level all the way. On July 5th, Gabriel wrote to his father from Recanati, telling him about the move and once more giving heartfelt advice for good Christian living.

On July 6th he set out once more.

This was Gabriel's good-bye to Recanati. He had passed through before on several occasions and he took with him in his mind's eye the image of the soft contours from the Cathedral to the hill known as "the Infinite" and the sudden rises in the curving streets that led to the city before dropping down to the sea. He had first come across this landscape on September 6-7, 1856 on the road from Spoleto to Morrovalle. No one knows how many times he stopped at Recanati while travelling on foot in pilgrimage to Loreto from Morrovalle, as the novices used to do. "He would sometimes pass through Recanati," explained Norbert, "on his way to Loreto." "Or arrangements were sometimes made for the Morrovalle novices to meet the Recanati students." The letter that Gabriel wrote to his cousin Peter of Terni, dated November 1, 1856, was sent from Recanati; however it is not known if this was another of Gabriel's stops in the city or if he had simply given the letter to someone else to mail, and it happened to be mailed from Recanati. The Church of the Passionist House in Recanati was known above all for its veneration of Our Lady of the Pietà, from which the Province received its name. For Gabriel, that mystery summed up the best of his life and of his plans.

And knowing Norbert, Gabriel, and the others, it is unimaginable that the group would have passed so close to Loreto without stopping there for Mass at the Holy House.

This was also Gabriel's good-bye to Loreto, the turning point of his devotion to Our Lady, the crucial link connecting Francis and Gabriel, the watershed between his life as a layman and as a Religious, where he had come out of the waters on one shore and immersed himself in the waters of the other shore. Gabriel's last Loreto prayer was joined to his first, and it is only right to respect its unutterable contents.

After the other stops along the way, Gabriel and company crossed the boundary between the Papal States and the Kingdom of Naples, at Martinsicuro, after the Tronto River, and entered Abruzzi.

This then was his good-bye to the Marches. Human designs had done so much to prolong his stay there, and even to try to bring him back there, but God had a different plan for him.

Chapter Twelve

Number One Again

Always the same thing: for a Passionist student, there is never anything new. School, studies, prayers, and a bit of relaxation, to share with others their studies and their prayers. If something ever did happen, it took place on a different level; you would have to look for it in the interior activity of the soul.

The trip to Isola del Gran Sasso came to a conclusion on July 10th, after a night spent in Giulianova and another in Montorio al Vomano. Gabriel had heard that the climate was better in Isola than in Pievetorina and that the place itself was very pleasant. No sooner did they arrive than he realized that this was true. He breathed more easily, his head felt lighter. He wrote to his father, quickly putting him at ease: "There are so many fruit trees, which makes me think that the climate here is very mild. And thanks be to God I am happy here. The air is excellent and the little headaches that I would often get in Pievetorina are now less frequent or have disappeared altogether. The people are very warm and friendly."

The Gran Sasso, the "Great Rock," was also there as an allurement that would never fade away. It almost seemed as if he could touch it with his hand and run among the clouds. It looked as though it were floating weightlessly in the air, but it was majestically set on the ground with its solemn procession of peaks. It entered into his very soul and became one with his desire to climb the heights of life.

This is the place where Gabriel would remain until his death; he would be here a total of two years and seven and a half months, without any noteworthy happenings except those that took place within. It is to these that we now turn our full attention.

Beautiful Within

To be very clear, we should specify here that we are not talking about "extraordinary" in the sense of spectacular or striking; it is true that Gabriel would sometimes like to be extraordinary in that sense, at least with regard to penitential practices, but he would give in to his director's good judgment and would desist. After all, the everyday life of the Passionist already had enough penitential practices, and in the end Gabriel would not even succeed in observing all of these. He would never do anything to be noted in public, rather he was very much opposed to any public displays. He would be heard to say that true greatness lay in the interior dispositions with which one worked, not in the quantity of works that one performed.

It was in his inner drive that he was exceptional. His greatness lay deep inside, in the strength of his love which would make its presence felt even in the smallest things. In this he never grew slack, and even if he were tired or sick, even in the face of temptation or when he was lacking motivation, he would not fail to love.

In the community he stood out, and was therefore always seen as special, though without any eccentricity. His was an extraordinary ordinariness, a capacity to live ordinary daily life with an extraordinary inner aptitude.

It was obvious that his attention was fully given to

something, and that this "something" filled him so completely that his thoughts were never removed from it, such that he barely even made a noise in the House. His awareness of the presence of God was so keen that he could not overlook it even for a moment. Meeting God and being with him became a part of everything he did and of everything that happened far or near. God had become his life and history.

His heart was "firmly set on God and fully immersed in him," even when he was studying or doing other things. This inner disposition was not something he had to consciously get himself to do, something that required effort such that the concentration could be seen on his face or that furrows would appear on his forehead; rather it was "the work of the heart that would totally involve his will and produce a spontaneous, gentle and effortless awareness in the mind, akin to an instinct that would satisfy some need of the soul." Living in this dimension, it is no wonder that one day he barely noticed that he had dropped a glass while at table and that it had broken.

A few months after he entered the Passionist House, it was already "possible to see that his life was a continual encounter with God." "At any moment you could ask him what he was thinking about, and he could always answer, 'God.'"

"His thoughts were in another world." "With his body he was here on earth, but with his mind he was in heaven"; this was the comment of Father Dominic Ciaranca, the country pastor of the parishes scattered about on the slopes of Gran Sasso, when he saw that Gabriel did not laugh at the jokes that were made when he would accompany the students on picnics in the mountains.

Norbert was certain that Gabriel had the special grace of self-knowledge or interior awareness because he was always able to "remain above himself."

This extraordinary inner awareness was evident above all in his prayer, which was the thing that "most strongly attracted him" and the thing that brought him greatest fulfillment. After praying or after receiving communion, he would sometimes become "radiant, flush with color and full of joy; other times pale, serious and in deep meditation." No sooner would he engage in prayer than he would suddenly find himself immersed "in a sea of pious thoughts." Every once in a while, the flood of feelings would surge out of control and external signs could be seen, such as the rocking of his head, tears, sudden flushes of color, heavy breathing. When these episodes would occur, whoever was next to him would try discreetly to call him back to himself. "God would sometimes come over him in a very strong way and, in a manner of speaking, in inopportune moments."

When he had just entered the novitiate, he was called upon to recite the meditation aloud, a practice commonly used with the novices to teach them how to pray. He was so good in his recitation that a Religious passing by the room paused for a long while at the door. He was Father Salviano Masolino, director of students in Recanati; he was out taking a walk and was at first drawn to the door out of curiosity but then remained there for edification.

Not only did Gabriel pray at the established times, but while he was doing other things he would prepare himself for prayer. His preparation included mortification, meditation and letting any news that might be a distraction fall by the wayside.

When speaking of his prayer, witnesses also commented that he had "a very special gift of God": that of being able to pray without distractions of any kind. In the past, the greatest feeling he would have was that of chasing after distractions; now he was a captive of his own inner being, because there he found God.

Assisi. *Above*: the Cathedral of Saint Rufinus. *Below*: the Town Square. The arrow to the left, on the municipal building, shows the house where Saint Gabriel of Our Lady of Sorrows was born; the arrow to the right shows where the family lived after they moved to the third floor of the facing Bozzoni Palace.

Assisi: the baptistery of the Cathedral. Saint Gabriel was baptized on the very day he was born (March 1, 1838) at the same font where Saint Francis and Saint Clare were baptized.

Spoleto: façade and bell-tower of the Cathedral.

The Passionist House of Morrovalle (in the province of Macerata) as it was at the time that Francis Possenti entered the novitiate. With his religious profession, he took the new name of Gabriel of Our Lady of Sorrows.

Caricatures of Francis' classmates, drawn by Francis Possenti when he was sixteen years old.

The sacred icon, a Byzantine image of Our Lady, kept in the Cathedral of Spoleto. During the procession of August 22, 1856, while he was looking upon the image, Francis Possenti felt the definitive call to Religious life.

Above: the Passionist House of Morrovalle as it looks today. *Below*: the retreat house of the Immaculate Conception in Isola del Gran Sasso as it looked in the days that Saint Gabriel lived there (1859 - 1862).

Two views inside the Shrine of Saint Gabriel (Isola del Gran Sasso). *To the side*: Saint Gabriel's place of burial beneath the church floor. *Below*: the chapel of Saint Gabriel (opened in 1920); beneath the altar is a bronze burial urn which contains Gabriel's remains.

On the following page: a panoramic view of the new Shrine of Saint Gabriel; in the background the old Basilica is visible.

Above: a close-up detail of Saint Gabriel's burial urn. *Below*: the "choir," that is, the internal chapel, of the Passionist House; in the niche is the statue of Our Lady of Sorrows that Saint Gabriel restored.

Above: the old Basilica of Saint Gabriel; the neo-classical façade is from 1929. *Below*: the soaring roof of the new Shrine; in the background is the massive rock formation of the Gran Sasso.

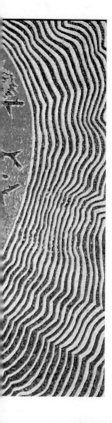

The Shrine of Saint Gabriel: two pieces of artwork by Ugolino da Belluno. *To the side*: a mosaic representing the Paschal mystery; the Crucified Lord and the Risen Christ (this latter after a painting by Pier della Francesca) are juxtaposed inside a heart surrounded by a line motif that produces a pulsating optical effect.

Below: stained glass window showing the parable of the Prodigal Son; the artist has included a feminine figure as a personification of the tenderness of God and a representation of the Church.

Three other pieces of artwork by Ugolino da Belluno as found in the new Shrine. *Above*: the heart-shaped bronze tabernacle (representing the sacrament of love and the emblem of the Passionists) buds forth from the center of a vine growing in the form of a cross. *Below*: the lectern with the inscription "The word of the Cross is the power of God"; on the wall, the table cloth spread out on a flowering field represents the multiplication of the loaves and fishes. *Facing page*: the bronze crucifix from the weekday chapel.

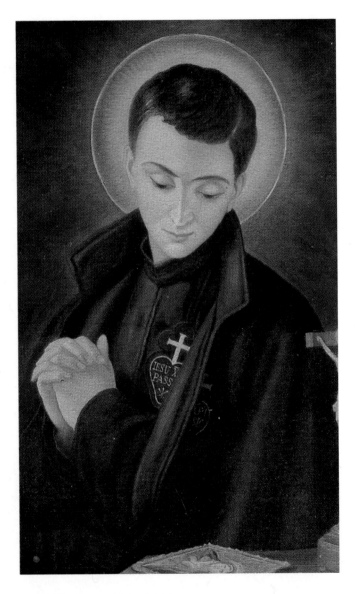

The traditional image of Saint Gabriel.

It Is Possible to Give More

His earlier talents had become virtues. Grace had taken possession of them and was developing them into heroic virtues for the good of the whole community.

God revealed himself to Gabriel's inner being in the mystery of the Crucified Lord. As a Passionist, the characteristics of the soul were formed through contemplation of the Cross of the Risen One, and everything else came from there as well: the consuming desire to imitate him in practicing virtue and in working for the salvation of others.

The Lord's Passion was the usual theme of meditation and conversation in the House among his companions. It would also be the center of the apostolic activity that they were preparing to become involved in. Gabriel spoke of the Passion "with much love and fervor." His spirituality was such that "it could be said that devotion to Christ Crucified was the queen and mother of every other devotion."

When a Passionist makes his Religious profession and takes vows, a Crucifix is given to him. This is the one thing that he can always take with him when he changes houses and when he goes to preach missions; when he dies, it is placed in his hands. This gesture says everything. The Crucifix becomes the Passionist's program for life. It is placed at the center of his desk and watches him while he studies and while he is in his room; it leaves the room with him and follows him when he goes out to preach; it calls him incessantly to examine his life in order to ensure that it is conformed to the Crucified Lord.

Gabriel too had his Crucifix and lived his life with it. He accepted the challenge to become himself "a little crucifix." He kept it before his eyes and would often kiss it. In this intimate encounter between Gabriel and the Crucified Lord was woven the mystery of Gabriel's life. No one knows what was said between them, what was given and what was received. The Crucified Lord is the irresistible invitation made to those who will not be satisfied with anything else. He is the final challenge made to those who long for greatness. Gabriel was one such person. He was great inside.

He made himself a paper copy of his Crucifix so that he could more easily take it with him and rest his eyes on it when he was at prayer, especially in the recitation of the Office, the celebration of Mass, and during periods of meditation.

Joined to the Crucifix, at the foot of the Cross, was an image of Our Lady of Sorrows, for, as Gabriel understood it, she was an essential element in the Passion of Jesus. Thus his whole life was permeated through and through by this atmosphere, and if one were to approach him, out would come the Crucified Lord and Our Lady of Sorrows.

He felt the living presence of the Crucified Lord in the Sacrament of the Eucharist. Someone said that his devotion to the Blessed Sacrament of the Altar was "perhaps more ardent" than that to the Crucified Lord. He often thought of the Blessed Sacrament and would visit it whenever he could. He would make use of the childlike custom found among some of the saints, that of sending his Guardian Angel to visit the Blessed Sacrament for him or that of leaving his heart behind in the Tabernacle. He would go round and round the Altar as though drawn by a magnet. The days of Communion were different from the other days; too bad there were only three such days a week! But like Saint Aloysius, he adopted the habit of dividing the time into two parts, the first being preparation and the second thanksgiving.

When it was his turn to take care of the Altar, he would prepare it to perfection; and if he found no flowers in the Passionists' garden, he would go pick some from the fields "with passion and joy" that were uncommon. If he knew that some priest was going to leave with Viaticum, he would ask permission to follow him. In Pievetorina, he went with Norbert when he brought communion to a Mrs. Marucci, and

he escorted the Eucharist to the bedside of the dying Brother
Michael. When out on walks, he would send greetings to
Jesus when he saw a church off in the distance.

The summit of his relationship with the Eucharist was
in the Mass, which he tried to attend as often as possible.
With his heart he would join himself to those Masses he could
not attend.

Devotion to the Sacred Heart of Jesus was growing
among the Passionists, thanks to Gabriel's influence. He had
learned this devotion from the Jesuits in Spoleto. From the
Passionist House he wrote several times to his family asking them to send him the booklets containing the history and
practices of this devotion; he was especially interested in
having those dealing with the Month of the Sacred Heart and
the Nine Offices of the Sacred Heart. After receiving them,
he distributed them among his confreres and among the few
people he would have occasion to meet.

Both his devotion to the Eucharist and to the Sacred
Heart became more intense in the period of the pre-Lenten
carnival, because he believed this period to be particularly
detrimental to the Christian life.

Among the different Saints, he was especially fond of
Aloysius Gonzaga, Francis of Assisi, Francis de Sales, Margaret of Cortona, Paul of the Cross and Saint Joseph, whom
he would call "my dear Saint Joe."

After he joined the Passionists, Gabriel's desire to succeed and achieve, so much a part of his personality, did not
diminish in the least. Quite the contrary: grace took firm hold
of this too and used it to produce great merits in holiness.
Christ's Passion had stimulated the imagination of his youth-
fulness. Prayer had become his preferred pastime and in
order that he might devote more time to praying well he
became less interested in other things. Being faithful to his
Religious vows and growing in virtue were the new areas of
interest and challenge in his young life.

He had always felt love for the poor, and now it had become part of his vow of poverty. He was happy that in the Religious family he had chosen, all were equal without any distinctions between them. Just about every time he wrote home he would recommend, especially to his father, that goods be shared with the poor; this should be done not so much as an act of compassion or generosity, but as an act of justice.

If he should meet a poor person while out on a walk, he would feel a special bond in the depths of his being and he would ask permission to speak words of comfort, to teach good rules of life, and to instill a sense of prayer. In Pievetorina, he would stand next to the Brother assigned to greet the poor who came to the door, and in a teasing manner he would say: I want to see your generosity! Then he would add: What a pittance, that won't even make it to his stomach! At meals there was the "mortification" plate, where the Passionists would put something for the poor; Gabriel would always put choice morsels because, as he would say, "it's not the leftovers that you should give to the poor."

In a year of famine, he was quick to spring into action, distributing foodstuffs to three hundred poor people. This immediately earned him the nickname "consoler of the poor." During the years of plundering he worked with Father Dominic Ciaranca distributing potatoes and portions of bread-soup to the people; Father Dominic had furnished himself with a large pot for the specific purpose of preparing these rations.

The poverty of life in community was not enough for him. "How poor are we really, when we lack nothing?" he would lament. For himself he would always choose and gather the poorest things, the most worn clothes, old pieces of thread to mend them, the crusts of bread. His director, a little to joke with him and a little to take him to task, reproached him: "How stingy; it's a good thing you didn't get married and let's hope they never make you Superior, otherwise I pity the person who will have to be at your side!"

But as much as he strove to be personally poor, to that same degree he was attentive that others should be lacking nothing. He was "all eyes to see the needs of others." "He could not bear to see those who had not voluntarily taken on a life of poverty suffer the difficulties and discomforts of being poor."

The wholesomeness in behavior and relationships that he had always observed had become now his vow of chastity. Focusing his energies on loving the Crucified Lord and Our Lady of Sorrows left no room for feelings or thoughts that for him would have been distracting. Norbert gives the assurance that "because of the intimate union he enjoyed with God" he never suffered failure in faithfulness to his vow of chastity, but he had to face a few strong episodes of temptation. Did he suffer from sexual frustration or repression? Had the vigor of his sexual drive atrophied? After all, even in the area of values, sexuality is a necessary component for self-affirmation.

The special qualities of his humanity did not wither away but were directed to a different level of fulfillment. The only faculty suspended was that of genitality and its corresponding physiological generative property. But this was not essential for personal fulfillment, for there were other ways of giving life. What was essential was to love, not to have sexual relations; to be life-giving, not to have children. Even today, burdening young people with the idea that they must marry at all costs, and teaching them that only through their relationship with their sexual partner can they find fulfillment, means perpetrating a fallacy in the transmission of information that is essential for choosing a vocation in life.

If sexuality is the mechanism that moves people out of themselves to others and makes them capable of loving, of giving themselves and giving life, then Gabriel had attained a fulfillment of himself that is markedly masculine and life-giving. In the Crucified Lord he found the limitless God to love and a limitless humanity to give himself to, for its salvation. The full spectrum of that love inherent in his sexual humanity filled every need and desire that he could have. His way of loving was welded, as it were, to Christ's way of loving. And he dared to love — God, man, the world, life, the things of everyday life — no longer with his heart alone but with God's heart, a result of the experience of consecrated chastity and of any authentic expression of Christian love.

The psychological equilibrium demonstrated by Gabriel and the joy of which he would continually speak and write was the proof that in chastity he had achieved full personal integration without the lack of anything and with nothing being out of balance.

His demand for freedom, already well used in the choices he had made, had become his vow of obedience. By means of this vow, he did not avoid responsibility or the risk involved in making decisions; rather, in faith and love, he entrusted himself to the Church, confident that through her mediation he would be guaranteed the best choices possible.

He did not suppress his own will, but made a gift of it to God. He wanted his own will to be that of God, which was revealed in the Church's authoritative discernment. For this reason he no longer trusted his own view of things but sought to learn those of his Superiors. "His will was that of his Superiors," in which he came to recognize the will of God. He was not interested in learning the reasons behind a "yes" or a "no"; he only wanted to know what the decision was. That was obedience.

It was not an act of the will only, but also an act of the intellect, agreeing to the view taken by the higher authority, and an act of faith.

As happens inevitably in community life, he would occasionally hear negative comments about the actions of one or another Superior. In such situations, as soon as he could, he would add his own comment, and it was always the same: "Well, one's own will is not pleasing to God. Even if one had the most convincing reasons and the holiest goals, one's own will is not pleasing to God — it just is not pleasing to him."

His insistent concern that everything turn out in the best way possible and that not even a moment of life be wasted had become self-abandon to God in faith and hope. Someone might ask him, what would you do if the novice master sent you back home? He would answer, I would place my trust in God. What would you do if they told you that you were dying? I would continue doing what I was doing at that moment, even if it were eating or sleeping.

The people of that day were in fact going through some dangerous times, running the risk even of death. They could hear the roar of the artillery during the battle of Civitella del Tronto. Around the Passionist House there were roving bands of reactionaries and brigands. One night they actually broke down the door and burst into the House. There were about sixty of them, armed to the teeth and looking for food. And there was in effect at that time a law that anyone caught giving them food would be sentenced to the firing squad. But Gabriel would calmly remark: "We are in God's hands." "It was as if there were nothing strange going on at all and everything was fine." And for several months these types of situations occurred almost everyday.

He knew how to perceive God's presence in the events of each day. He was able to see God everywhere and in everything; "a flower, a piece of fruit, and every other thing was like a mirror where he saw the reflection of God and God's perfection." Every creature was "an easy and comfortable path leading to God." He felt attracted to nothing other than "to supernatural goods and virtue." "His thoughts were always centered on the things of God."

He did feel the need to work for salvation without wasting any time. He used to say: let's not stand around with our hands in our pockets! He would quote Saint Philip Neri: "Heaven is not made for lazy-bodies." At the same time, giving himself in complete abandon to God made him feel certain of salvation, to the point that Norbert was worried that

he might be committing the sin of presumption. But Norbert
was reassured when he realized that Gabriel's certainty
came from the Crucified Lord and Our Lady of Sorrows. "If
salvation were in our hands, then we would indeed have
every reason to tremble."

These virtues came from God; therefore he would prepare himself to receive them through prayer, through theological and Biblical studies, and through wholesome reading material. His prayer books and textbooks were filled with
pieces of paper on which were written Bible verses or useful
reflections that he would gather wherever he could: from
meditations, from sermons, from his confreres; they were like
energy pills to keep his spiritual life going strong.

His sociableness and ability to establish contacts had
become Christian charity, which allowed him to enter into
communion with all people.

He was able to see every person "in God and in relationship to God." He responded well to the challenge Christ
put to his disciples, to see him in others. He brilliantly tack-
led the test of being able to see in every man and woman of
this world the hidden incarnation of the God who was one
with humanity. A test which is a challenge and a trap for
every Christian.

Gabriel had succeeded here also: in him there was no
envy or jealousy, nor bitterness or grumbling, but only charity that was able to understand everything. He did not overlook even the slightest need of others, despite the mock re-
bukes of his director: "What a nosey-body; why don't you
mind your own business!" As for himself, he was quite content if no one paid any heed to him at all. They called him
"mother to everyone."

He did not allow himself to be judgmental. He once con-
fessed to a confrere: "Three times I made a poor judgment,
and three times I was guilty of the same mistake." He promised Our Lady that he would "not criticize anyone even if the
case were clear and evident." He would not tolerate talking

ill of others, whether they were present or absent, living or dead; not even of the brigands who broke into the House or of those who were of a different school of thought or belief. He could be aggressive, however, when it was a question of defending someone's reputation.

For him, all people were equal and he would not let himself be swayed by sympathy. If he did have a preference, it was for those whom he saw as more isolated or whom he found it more difficult to be with.

So as not to make his schoolmates feel bad, in scholastic debates he would not pursue the issue when they were short of arguments. When making the Passionist symbol for his habit, he would exchange his, done to perfection, with that of some confrere whose work left something to be desired.

He was good even at the smallest things that drew attention precisely because of their littleness: he knew how to thank people, how to smile, how to say a kind word to those who were down, how to put aside some of the cherries for the confrere who was out, how to make things easier for those who had received some penance to do.

He would ask for forgiveness the minute he even suspected that someone might be unhappy with him, even to the point of exaggeration, making the other remark ironically: I won't forgive you because you haven't done anything to upset me! His humility, however, was quite genuine: he would say, "Don't imitate me because I always give a bad example!"

These are all subtle things, but in putting together a picture of Gabriel they are all essential.

He Remains a Leader

He had always been deeply intuitive and was able to communicate with sincerity. Now this ability became a means of apostolate, which is nothing more than living the experience of God and awakening it in others or transmitting it to others. He was preparing himself for the Passionist apostolate in the ministry of priesthood, but in the meantime he did not just stand around doing nothing. He was already a missionary with his whole life.

First of all by example. When a guest from outside would come to stay at the Passionist House for a period of reflection, he would realize immediately that Gabriel was someone who understood God and was on very familiar terms with him; and he would ask Gabriel to talk to him about God. Just looking at him was enough to awaken in people the desire to be virtuous. "He was so focused on God and united with him that just looking at him would help you to refocus your own life and fill you with strong emotion." His confreres would look to him to remind themselves how they should be: "This confrere of mine was an angel come down from heaven in the flesh."

His example was most powerful when he was praying. He looked like a statue. When he went to receive Holy Communion or when he gave thanks afterward he actually transmitted his fervor to others and made any desire for distraction disappear. The same was true when he was at Mass. The faith and devotion that possessed him could be seen in his face, so much so that the townspeople would notice it and stop just to watch "the little saintly Brother." "It was beautiful watching him pray," summarized his confrere Bernardo Silvestrelli. When he would get sick, being present at his prayer was touching: "I am not exaggerating when I say that he would bring tears to people's eyes, and move their heart to devotion. I saw people who were not so devout come to see him, and they were visibly moved and had tears in their eyes," commented Norbert.

Then there were his walks. Among the Passionists of that time, a walk was part of the structure of their life, otherwise it would have been impossible to endure the stark-

ness to which they were committed. There was an hour of
walking each day, divided into two parts; it was called a soli-
tary walk and had to be taken in silence. But when he was
sick, Gabriel received permission to speak with the hired
help and with the boys who visited the House, to better take
his mind off his illness. Once a week there was a half-day
walk for the whole community all together, and another
shorter community walk on Sunday afternoons, after Benediction. Once a month, when the weather was good, there
were also special whole day walks, with a sack lunch.

These outings became a training course for Gabriel in
his apostolate of giving good example and speaking of God.
It was on these occasions that the most interesting little
episodes took place, episodes that people would later recount.
When goodness is present, it cannot be hidden; there was
no sense in trying to pretend that it was not there. The people
would remember him as "the one who was modest and went
about with his head bowed." When people would come across
him "they admired his exceptional modesty and concentration as he would always go about with his head bowed."
There would usually be someone who would be very moved,
and some young man would see him and would feel the desire to become a Religious himself.

At some point, it became clear to the watchful eyes of
the highland townsfolk that Gabriel's health was declining.
In Fano a Corno, seeing that he would always arrive last and
out of breath, they would wonder: "If it is so difficult for him,
why do they bring him along?" In Casale di San Nicola they
would ask: "What's he trying to do, this little Brother who
just isn't up to all this anymore?", and they put him on a mule
so he could arrive with the others at the little hillside chapel
near the Gran Sasso.

Among his confreres too he was esteemed. They would
gladly listen to him, they would pay much attention to his
insistence on the importance of devotions; they had agreed
to point out each other's shortcomings, but they never found

any in him. They would recall: "You would never grow tired of dealing with him, his company was always pleasant and brought relief." "Listening to him was inspiring." "I felt a new fervor of spirit arise in me and my will to practice virtue was enflamed."

Conversations were centered on spiritual themes and it seemed that there was nothing to think about except God. Norbert would point out still another "special grace" received by Gabriel: he would never get carried away in his speech. Something he had never seen, Norbert would say later as an old man, after much experience as a spiritual director and as one responsible for evaluating candidates for priesthood.

Among the customs of the Passionists in training the younger members in the art of communication was the "reflection," a type of small sermon given to the community soon after lunch and after supper. In this custom Gabriel found a golden opportunity to convey the love he lived.

The contents of his apostolate were those of his life itself: the Crucified Lord, Our Lady of Sorrows, the will of God, devotions. To young people he would meet in the Passionist House or out on walks, he would encourage obedience to parents and he would teach them the Hail Mary and how to meditate on the Lord's Passion and on Our Lady of Sorrows. His ability to teach Christian doctrine and moral conduct could be seen from the dedication with which he studied them himself and with which he would undertake to instill them in others in conversations during his walks, in his exhortations to the community, and in the public preaching that would be assigned to him for practice.

Any time is a good time for doing good. It happened that Francis Dionisi, a student with Masonic sympathies, was sent to the Passionist House as a punishment by his uncle, the pastor of Isola del Gran Sasso, with whom he was taking private lessons. Gabriel was happy to stay with him; he gave him encouragement and congratulated him when he learned that he planned on becoming a doctor. He wished him well with his studies, which would be long; he knew because he had a brother who was studying medicine. He regretted that when he finally did become a doctor, he would not be around any more. But his principal intent was to convince him that he should study philosophy in the seminary, because other schools did not deal with the problem of the soul and were infected with Giobertian philosophy. A Freemason was not able to understand how a person could last month after month in a Religious House. Gabriel explained: "When you think of the eternity of paradise, days go by as if they were just brief moments."

In the community there were Religious who spent their lives going off to preach according to the Passionist style. They would preach on the Crucified Lord, the eternal truths, the great questions of life, and they would obtain even astonishing conversions. These Passionists, when they would return to the House to replenish their strength and charge themselves up again before the Crucified Lord, were invited by the director to tell the students about their experiences. For Gabriel, these were moments that filled him to overflowing with enthusiasm; with eyes wide open, he dreamt of becoming just like them, and wanted to do so as soon as possible. He liked to think that there would be no limit to the different areas where he would exercise his apostolate. He did not exclude the possibility of preaching among those who were not yet converted to the faith; in fact he felt an acute kind of envy for the missionaries who were fortunate enough to go abroad to preach the Gospel. "To those poor souls," he would say speaking about the pagans, "I would like to introduce my Mother."

Even his letters tell us much about the adventure he was living. They are not masterpieces of literature or theology, but they do reveal the contentedness of a satisfied life and his intense concern for his father's and brothers' spiritual life. In his letters he would continually mention devotion to Our Lady, taking care of the poor, regret for the pleasures he engaged in as a boy, the Christian life and the salvation of those to whom he wrote.

Initially he felt that writing often was a burden because it was a distraction, but then he realized that letter-writing gave him a way to tend to the souls of his family; therefore he would regularly write lengthy exhortations to them. Many of the letters never arrived; perhaps they were seized because of the political censorship going on at the time and they might still be laying in some forgotten storage area. But the letters that we do have are enough to give a good picture of this aspect of his apostolate. "I can't make you understand how much I desire the eternal salvation of my brothers; therefore may they go often to the Sacraments, may they flee bad company and be submissive and obedient." "After the salvation of my own soul, I ask for that of yours and of my brothers, and of the whole household... of all of my brothers and sisters, for whose eternal salvation I am always fearful; I would like to see them all one day safely in port."

The intensity of his feelings in this regard can be seen in the special language that he used when addressing this issue. He would always talk about speaking "with his heart" or "with his heart in his hand" or "with his heart in the pen" or "with his heart on his lips."

The remainder, and the greater part, of Gabriel's missionary nature was expressed in his desire for and union with God. Identifying himself with the Crucified Lord, he filled himself, as much as his being could hold, with the Lord's own love. In that love he could reach all people and respond to all the sighs of humanity for salvation. But the fruits of this apostolate are beyond our knowledge and are still being produced.

Chapter Thirteen

You Need Love

"I feel unable to tell you even one per cent." "If I had to tell everything, I would never finish." "It is impossible to say how tender and sincere his love for her was and how completely possessed by her his heart was." "He was like dough kneaded through and through by love for Our Lady." Devotion like that, "so loving, active, generous, constant, resourceful, I had never seen nor heard of nor read about."

The adventure of Gabriel with Mary the Mother of God and of all humanity is the area that Norbert felt least capable of talking about. We can attribute this in part to the hagiographic emphasis of the director-admirer of Gabriel in his testimony for Gabriel's cause of canonization. But here we are entering into the very depths of Gabriel's inner being.

Accustomed as we are to distorted relationships between the sexes, and ready to see the treacherous workings of the unconscious in just about everything, it is difficult for us to accept the enchanting relationship between Gabriel and Mary without being somewhat suspicious of it. How can we not think in terms of some compensatory mechanism, or just plain soppy sentimentality, in a young man who was not yet fully mature?

Nevertheless, Gabriel's experience showed characteristics of a mature awareness. Obviously, this maturity took time to develop fully. Gabriel experienced this relationship on the psychological level of an orphan in need of motherly affection; he turned to Our Lady as to a mother, employing the familiar language that a child would use, corresponding to the developmental stages of his age. There is nothing strange in this, all the more so since the focus of his attention is Our Lady of Sorrows, which did not allow a sentimental or effeminate love. We can also admit that in his formation there was a maternal role played by the dynamic presence of our Heavenly Mother.

He drew inspiration and strength from the Marian doctrines of the time, based on the anthologies of the Fathers and on the examples given by the Saints, and filled with devotional practices. But, from an ecclesiastical point of view and from a Passionist perspective, his was a unique experience.

Gabriel's devotion to Mary was rooted in the heart of his own mother Agnes. Even if this occurred initially without his being aware of it, it was natural that he should move from the sorrow of losing his mother to a great devotion to our Mother of Sorrows. This devotion became stronger as he prayed before the sculpture of the Pietà in the Possenti home; profound traces of his interiorization of those moments of prayer can be found in the advice he would often give from the Passionist House: do not forget that statue. "I would like you to show it respect; if you want to remember me, it is enough that you do this." "I recommend that you spend time before the little statue of Mary, Our Sorrowful Lady." "If you ever change houses, don't forget the statue..." "How do you honor that image of Our Lady?"

There was also his father's example. Besides praying before the statue of the Pietà at home, he would make daily visits as well to the Church of Saint Luke where the image of Our Lady of Sorrows was venerated. The family's Marian devotion was evident in yet another way, in the daily recitation of the rosary. From Morrovalle, Gabriel would write of his regret for "playing or sleeping or doing other things" at times, while the family was praying the rosary. This devotion, however, left its mark on him.

These initial traits became the basic structure and developed into a personal spirituality in Spoleto, under the direction of the Jesuits in the Sodality of Mary.

Nor should the influence of the Servants of Mary be discounted. In Italy these Religious men were the principal agents for spreading the devotion to Our Lady of Sorrows. In Spoleto, they were the ones who took care of the Church of Saint Luke, where they had formed a group of lay people dedicated to the Seven Sorrows of Mary with special devotional practices during the month of May.

Some decisive event must have also taken place in the Holy House of Loreto. Gabriel was at the turning point from the lay life to the Passionist life, and he visited the Holy House at more or less the same time that preparations were being made for his entrance into society by becoming engaged to get married. His psychological development had reached the stage where he felt that he was no longer a little boy who needed his mother but a man who was ready to marry. From that moment on his devotion to Mary took on a more mature aspect than it had had in the past; it had become the conscious center of his spiritual life.

From Morrovalle on this devotion becomes characteristic of Gabriel. In five and a half years he will develop from it an exemplary lifestyle.

In Morrovalle he found the proper environment to grow in his pious fascination for Mary, thanks to the Passionist training in Marian devotion that had been developed by the novice master Father Raphael and by the assistant novice master Father Norbert. The doctrinal sources of this training were *The Glories of Mary* by Saint Alphonsus Liguori, *The Love of Mary* by the Camaldolese hermit Father Robert, and the Passionist tradition itself that was handed down from the founder Saint Paul of the Cross.

With the move to Father Norbert as his director this

characteristic of Gabriel's became accentuated. Norbert, a young man himself who had also been called to the Passionists by the internal mediation of Our Lady, was writing a new treatise on Mariology, the contents of which he would share in the classroom during the students' lessons. Gabriel's energetic affection was thus given a theological framework.

Our Lady was permanently present in his heart. Gabriel writes down the fundamental resolution of his life: "I will never refuse anything that is asked of me for love of Mary," which, rendered in a spirited slogan for all occasions became: "Gabriel, won't you win for love of Mary?"

He was "a fire of love" for her. In speaking about her "he always found new things to say." Although he might have soon run out of things to say when talking about other matters, when talking about Our Lady he was "profuse, insatiable."

Michael Tudini, a classmate, once heard him speak of Our Lady more passionately than usual. While he was trying to follow the course of what was being said, he saw a flame flash out from Gabriel's heart and dissipate as it flared toward him. From that moment he too felt ablaze with devotion to Our Lady and for the rest of his life there remained with him the sensation of the flame that had touched him.

To a colleague who asked Gabriel if he was not exaggerating, he responded: "You do me too much honor. This is nothing compared to what I could say." He did not tolerate "that others should be lacking," that is weak in their love of Our Lady.

He preferred preachers who spoke of Mary. He always enjoyed hearing of miracles, conversions and apparitions in which she was instrumental.

In the attic of the Passionist House in Isola there was an abandoned statue of Our Lady of Sorrows that the missionaries used to take with them when they went preaching. Gabriel decided that, with a little bit of restoration, it could still be used to inspire devotion. He gave himself to that task with an artistic sense marked by love. He put the folds back in the robes, applied varnish to the face so as to give it the look of anguish, carved a new wooden sword and placed it with trepidation on her heart, and then put the statue on display in the place of community prayer.

From Pievetorina on, he no longer wrote of Our Lady alone, but always mentioned her together with Christ. He probably did the same in talking about her, which is a sign that his Marian consciousness was becoming more finely tuned and growing deeper.

He placed unlimited trust in Our Lady. He was certain that devotion to her diminished the sufferings of death, "when we have our soul in our teeth," as he would say. He believed that it was possible for her to come and meet those who are dying, as different saints were reported to have experienced. With his love for her, he felt peace even regarding the problem of predestination, which at that time was a cause of worry for many students of theology. Whenever any problem or difficult situation arose in his young adulthood, his energetic response was always the same: "Dearest Mother, take care of it."

When visiting churches during his walks, he would pray before the tabernacle, and afterward he would go looking for the altar of Our Lady. If the image of Mary was "well made," everything was fine; if, however, it was "poorly executed," he was capable of crying out: Dearest Mother, how ugly they've made you!

In the Passionist House, he wanted to take care of the altar of Our Lady himself. He tended a special flower bed so he would always have fresh flowers. In winter he would use flowerpots that he kept protected from the cold. When there were no more of his flowers, he would go looking for some or asking for them out in the country. One time a young shepherd boy of Fano a Corno made him very happy by bringing a bouquet of violets.

The Marian feastdays would find him more involved than usual. He would increase not only his devotions, but especially his commitment to prayer and to practicing virtue. He would prepare himself for each feast with a novena, or at least a triduum; for the Feast of the Assumption he observed a special forty-day period of preparation. If you were to add up all the Marian feastdays (between simple and solemn ones, there were at that time twenty-seven listed in the calendar), the triduums and novenas, plus the month of May and that of September (for the seven sorrows of Mary; at that time, it was not yet the custom to set aside the month of October for the rosary): all told, there would remain very few days of the year that did not have a particular "Marian" character.

Perhaps as a result of helping Norbert put together the course on Mariology, which meant spending some time summarizing the contents of *The Glories of Mary* and following his own instincts with regard to his personal devotion to Our Lady, he wrote a little personal tract of theology and faith concerning Our Lady; it was entitled *A Marian Profession of Faith*. It became very important to him because in its pages he had distilled his own spiritual experience. He would have liked to have written it with his own blood, so intimately bound did he feel to what was expressed in it. But the text was quite long, and he was not sure how to ask the director's permission. In fact, Norbert's response was: "Don't even think of it!"

This Marian profession of faith, or "creed," does not really have a particular literary or theological value, but it does have a fundamental spiritual importance for understanding Gabriel. He would always keep it with him, at least part of it, for it was the mystery of his soul put into words.

His day was filled with various acts of devotion to Our Lady. He greeted her with a Hail Mary as he went into or came out of his room, and when the clock struck. He always wore his rosary beads from his belt and put them around his neck when he went to bed.

For him, Mary was above all Our Lady of Sorrows. This was how he always related to her and was the reason for which he also took that title as part of his own Religious name. Our Lady of Sorrows was not a woman overcome by desperation who collapsed into an emotional heap because of her pain; instead she was the one who "stood" at the foot of the Cross without fear. She was the personification of love's suffering; love that did not flee from suffering but which took this suffering upon itself, sharing in the suffering of others, whether it was the suffering of her Son on the Cross or the suffering of any man or woman in their humanity.

Just a few months after his entrance into the novitiate, it seemed that he thought of nothing except Our Lady of Sorrows and that he did not wish to speak of anything else. Give him an opening and he would become like "kindling set ablaze." On Saturdays, instead of meditating on the Passion, the Passionists would meditate on Heaven. They would ask Gabriel how his meditation on Heaven went and he would answer: "My Heaven is the suffering of my dear Mother." He took it upon himself at the beginning of each month to assign to each of his fellow students one of the sufferings of Our Lady to meditate on; this was all the more proper since for a certain period of time the group consisted of exactly seven.

To the four vows he had taken as a Religious and as a Passionist he wanted to add a fifth personal vow, the vow to spread devotion to Our Lady of Sorrows. "Practically his whole life he would pester me" about doing this, Norbert reported. Three times Norbert denied him permission, then two times he allowed him to make such a vow for a year, and finally he granted permission for him to make a permanent vow — but it was already Autumn of 1861.

Our Lady of Sorrows and the Crucified Lord were becoming so interconnected in his experience that he felt as though they were but two sides of the same mystery, two aspects that were interchangeable or that could be superimposed, one on the other. Just as the Crucified Lord summed up the all-encompassing mystery of Christ, so Our Lady of Sorrows was the most comprehensive title for the mystery of Mary, embracing everything from the Annunciation to Calvary.

Bernard Silvestrelli, a fellow novice, has left us an account that perfectly describes Gabriel's Marian spirituality: Gabriel would contemplate Christ's Passion as it was reflected in the heart of Mary; he would place himself in Mary's heart in order to contemplate Christ's Passion from her perspective. Looking upon the Crucified Lord with the heart and from within the heart of his Mother, he would also feel Mary's pain and would find his life spiritually placed within the unique mystery of the redemptive and co-redemptive suffering-love of the Son and his Mother.

When a spiritual experience leads to a life conformed to that of Christ, which is the vocation of every baptized person, there can be no doubt as to its theological correctness. This was the case with Gabriel's experience of Mary. Bernard went on to explain: "To please Mary," Gabriel succeeded in every undertaking: he left his own judgments and will aside so that he could be shaped and molded; he kept his heart in check so as not to waste love; he courageously faced every difficulty, suffering, annoyance and temptation; in a word, to the degree that was possible for him, he became an image of Jesus.

It could not be any clearer. Norbert himself would sum up: Our Lady was the "principal motivation" of Gabriel's whole life. She began her work in him at Spoleto, accompanied him and continued her work in him while he was with the Passionists, and she brought this work to completion when she finally came to take him.

Gabriel confided to his director that there had been six key incidents that marked his life, binding it in a special way to the presence of Our Lady; the seventh was his death. Thus there was a certain parallel with the seven sufferings of Mary. It is too bad that his director no longer remembered what these key happenings were. It is useless trying to guess the secrets of the soul, but certainly the list of events would have included Spoleto on August 22nd and Loreto on September 8th, both in the year 1856.

The Christian mystery is like a chain: take hold of one link and you bring along all the others. One's spirituality can be founded on the Baby Jesus, the Crucified Christ or the Risen Lord; on the Eucharist or the Church or Mary. Everything is joined together and leads to the other aspects of the one mystery of Christ, Crucified and Risen from the dead.

A Marian spirituality does not mean a Mary-centered spirituality, because the center is always Christ. It means "the light in which" the experience of salvation is experienced and lived; it is the perspective that colors the particular way in which we relate to God and to others as we yield to the love that saves us and makes us co-workers in the plan of salvation.

Gabriel saw all this and lived it in Mary's motherhood and universal mediation. He experienced and showed that from the moment of the Incarnation, the coming of Christ, the Savior of all men and women, occurs through the mediation of his Mother; this was what God had willed. And Christ's coming in history is what makes present-day men and women holy.

Chapter Fourteen

The Danger of Going Too Fast

Always giving his all, full of spunk, never missing a beat. He was as he had always been, driven to outdo and surpass everyone else. How long could he go on like this?

He faced two great dangers in his life: that of not making up his mind in time — if he had missed his calling, he would have become someone else, not Gabriel; and that of giving too much of himself all at once — he took off like a rocket, but that is not the way to climb a mountain. What would happen if he failed?

He was not content just to be a good person. He had made the choice to go for it all. He went from being comfortable with all kinds of possibilities before him, to being someone who had nothing, not even a flower that he could give to his brother; from being an extraordinary speaker, to being someone who could move others to tears by talking about the Crucified Lord or Our Lady of Sorrows; from being a good-looking, dashingly dressed young man to being a Passionist Brother clothed in an unstylish all-one-piece habit, with his hair cut short and bare feet that would become chapped and cracked in the winter; from being an exuberant and sparkling fellow to being a silent and sighing contemplative; from being a lover of entertainment to being someone who had fallen in love with the sacrifice of giving his life; from being a future spouse and father of a family to being someone pledged to humanity, who wished to save others with the longing that is born of Calvary; from being a seeker of the distractions of the dance floor to being someone whose efforts were focused on his own interior life; from being someone who used sweet-talk to get what he wanted to being someone who used his persuasive powers to get people to love Our Lady; from being someone who was restless and tormented, never in peace, to being someone who was calm and satisfied, always at peace "within these sacred walls"; from being someone who was the picture of health to being someone who had become weak and was lacking in stamina; from being Francis the lady's man to being Gabriel of Our Lady of Sorrows. Before, he bided his time and put things off; now, he was all anticipation and anxious eagerness to go.

He would even walk fast; he wanted always to forge ahead.

His impatience to become like the Crucified Lord led him to come up with ingenious ways of increasing his penitential practices. Of the forty resolutions that he had written for himself in order to keep himself in the spirit of self-denial from the first year, almost all of them had to do with sacrifices to be made during the day. In the last of these resolutions he dared to impose on himself to avoid any failure.

Norbert's greatest difficulty in directing him was keeping him from going overboard on the privations that he wanted to inflict on himself, otherwise "in just a short time he would ruin his health." He was able to put together clever ruses that were so subtle and sly that if Norbert did not keep a sharp lookout he would easily fall for them and agree to what Gabriel was asking so as to appease him. Norbert was able to keep him under control for a time by explaining the concept of double merit: if Gabriel was obedient, he would gain merit because he was giving up his own will, and he would also gain merit because he was offering up the sacrifices that he had wanted to make. But after a while, it all seemed too easy to Gabriel. He believed that only difficult things were truly meritorious, only those things that you felt in your own flesh like the nails of the Cross. In this area he always showed an unstable nature, because he had "an inclination to excess." Only obedience saved him. His fellow student Brother Silvester would be shocked by this attitude of his: "In mortification he would often go beyond the limit," so much so that the director would have to step in and monitor him.

When he was at home with his family, everyone knew what a sweet tooth he had; among the Passionists no one ever suspected. The same thing with fruit: he would always prefer to refuse it in order to make a small sacrifice. And he was very happy with the Passionist custom of making sacrifices for the forty days preceding the feast of the Assumption: these days always came at the height of the heat of summer. The intermediate recipient of all these gifts was always Our Lady, to whom he would present them "like a garland."

Another concern of his that bordered on obsession was his devotional practices. Just the list of those that he would engage in every day is enough to boggle the mind: how could he ever have had time to do anything else? In honor of Our Lady, there were rosaries, chaplets to Our Lady of Sorrows and the Immaculate Conception; seven Hail Marys to Our Lady of Sorrows, often with his arms outstretched in the form of a cross; Hail Marys were also said going to and fro from his room, when the clock chimed at quarter hour intervals, and at the beginning of any activity; the Angelus three times a day with the community; the *Stabat Mater* — when he recited this during illness, "it seemed that he wanted to breathe his last breath with Our Lady."

In honor of Christ Crucified there was the Way of the Cross, "not a printed version, but one with great personal feeling." Of itself, the day was already focused on Christ's Passion, from meditation to community discipline and practices.

With regard to the Blessed Sacrament of the Eucharist, he would make visits whenever he could and would make frequent spiritual communions. He participated in sacramental communion and Mass with heartfelt devotion according to the spirituality of the day.

To the Sacred Heart of Jesus he would make nine offices together with his fellow students; there was also the chaplet to the Sacred Heart: if he had not said it by day's end, he would recite it under the light in the corridor or in the director's room, since the students' room had no lights. For Saint Joseph there was the chaplet of the seven joys every day, with the "Wednesdays" and the "Six Sundays."

In the Passionist House he kept a record of the confraternities he had belonged to as a boy in Spoleto, and he added a few others, always remaining faithful to the various practices and duties that were incumbent upon the members. These included the Sodality of Mary, the Confraternities of Our Lady of Mount Carmel, of Our Lady of the Holy Rosary, of Our Lady of Sorrows, of the Sacred Heart of Jesus, of the Most Precious Blood, and of Saint Margaret of Cortona of Monsanpietrangeli in the Marches.

Then he would speak once more against those who practice many devotions but without really being aware of what they are doing. He would say: "Little and well: it is better to say one Hail Mary with true devotion than a thousand without devotion." Norbert would later comment: his devotional practices would have been a great weight "to someone who did not really have devotion."

In his letters, Gabriel felt that he was a missionary sent to preach the importance of devotional practices, especially of those to Our Lady; these were always part of his passionate spiritual advice: "How many are they who, with seven Hail Marys, with a *Stabat Mater*, with a rosary, a short office or some other devotion, have been snatched from the grasp of the devil," or "have truly become saints." "Whatever the cost or sacrifice, never ever neglect the practice of the devotions that you have committed yourself to in honor of the Most Blessed Virgin Mary." "I beseech you never to neglect the rosary and *Stabat Mater* even at the cost of your very life."

It was typical that the spirituality of the day be nourished by and expressed in devotional practices. It is true that charity, and not devotional practices, make people holy. However, until the Second Vatican Council, the currents of Christian spirituality would flow in the streams of devotions. They were very much practiced even among lay people, especially those dedicated to the Blessed Virgin Mary. Nineteenth century Italy was known as the land of Our Lady. Such devotional practices were commendable because they were sometimes the only way of preserving and passing on the faith, even if there was the danger that they could make the faith seem private and evasive. In our modern day, the place of these devotions has largely been taken over by the prominence given to the Bible and the Liturgy, and by the commitment to works of social charity. But they still have an important role to play in the spiritual life. Gabriel brought many of his devotional practices with him from home, coming from Spoleto, and had the opportunity to evaluate them and increase them with the Passionists.

Gabriel's spiritual fervor includes every area of his life. He gave his all to everything and in a very single-minded way: he wanted all sin, even the smallest, out of his life. "Nothing to offend God ever." There was but one thing that caused him fear: "to despise or offend God even in the least." There was never a need to urge him to do better, but just the opposite: it was necessary to keep him from going overboard. He did everything as if it were the last thing he would ever do, as if afterward would come his meeting with God. In every moment he was filled to overflowing and in every action he gave every bit of himself.

Having impulsively given himself over to this way of living, he would maintain this pace and not slow down at all. Norbert would often ask himself if there were something more that could be desired, if there were some virtue that

Gabriel lacked; he had to always answer no. "I don't remember him ever not doing what he was supposed to do. I don't remember even one single time that he deliberately committed even the smallest offense. I don't remember him ever giving in to passion. I don't remember him ever having any doubt about having been faithful to chastity."

Gabriel got it in his head to take another vow: the vow to behave always in the most perfect way possible. "Time and time again he pleaded with me and insisted that I let him take this vow; he stopped only when he saw that I was firmly resolved not to give in to him, and he accepted my advice to put such behavior into practice but without taking a vow. And that's exactly what he did, without the least trouble or scruple."

He was not one who did God's work only part-time, but full-time, all the time. If there were anything that seemed to invite the total and complete giving of himself, he would certainly fall in love with it. Ever since the novitiate he had committed himself to the "heroic act," or the vow of purgatory, which consisted in renouncing the merits of one's own life in order to direct them to the benefit of the poor souls in purgatory. Besides he was convinced that "Our Lady will take care of me."

There were nonetheless two things that Norbert felt could possibly lead him astray: "his attachment to penitential practices and his attachment to certain pious practices that he had committed himself to." But again obedience saved him. In February of 1861 Norbert sent word to Sante that: "Gabriel's behavior is exceptional, nor do I have to correct him except in the excess of his fervor."

Norbert's observations are in line with those of the community. Francis Xavier del Principe, "the fellow student in whom he confided with greatest intimacy," would relate: "I never saw in him any defect or voluntary imperfection." Norbert had no doubts: "A life of holiness and innocence not only to the point of being unable to commit a single sin, but

such that not even the least conscious defect can be found"
is the highest grace he received through Our Lady.

Two facts vividly give the sense of Gabriel's intense commitment to the utmost.

In his room he was immersed as usual in the desire to
give himself totally to the Lord. A footstep and the rustling
sound of the habit told him that the director was passing
down the corridor. He opened the door, called the director
into the room and threw himself to his knees, pleading as if
some great weight were upon him: "Tell me, Father, please,
if there is anything in my heart that is displeasing to God!
Please tell me because I want to tear it out!" While saying
this, he moved his hands to his chest as if searching out his
heart, making a gesture as if he were tearing something out.

During recreation time, the students would get together
in groups of two and talk about their classes or interior experiences. Gabriel burst into tears before his fellow student
while he was telling him about the strong attraction he felt
to God and about his sadness in feeling that he was not a
saint: "I experience such strong inner feelings, God wants
me to be completely his, but I am not!" And down came the
tears, embarrassing his fellow student but also leaving him
full of admiration.

In these tears and in this gesture of removing from his
heart all that is displeasing to God, we find the Gabriel who
moved along at full speed, who never slowed down. The only
danger was that his motor would not be able to withstand
the strain.

Chapter Fifteen

Things to Laugh at or to Think About

He took sharp aim against the world: "The miserable and fleeting pleasures that it gives are laced with an infernal poison." "Some companions with the nicest ways about them lead us directly to hell." "The theater, useless conversation: goodness, how those things make me groan! I would have fallen into an abyss if Mary hadn't come running to save me. Those things were death-dealing for me." "Flee bad company. Flee the theater: if you are in a state of grace before God when you go into the theater, it is difficult to come out without having lost that grace or without having endangered it. Flee useless conversation. Flee bad books, those accursed novels; I weep and sigh: if only I had never read them! They seemed innocent but they were so full of the devil; they were causing my heart to rot." "The world is a traitor." "Flee idleness and wretched pastimes; what distasteful things these are for me." And to his brother who was a priest, "Flee idle conversation with women."

In regard to his great zeal for mortification, today we might suspect that it was unhealthy. Not only was he enamored of mortification, but he seemed starved for it and found ways to make it a part of everything: of his eating, drinking, sleeping, speaking, sitting, standing, and even his walks. "He would have become a martyr" by dint of strict discipline, hairshirts, the little chains he would wear and other tools from his arsenal of mortification. He went to see his sister Teresa and did not even speak to her until his director remembered to give him permission to do so. On the trip to the Cathedral of Penne to receive minor orders, he would never raise his eyes at the stop-overs where benefactors offered them lodging. The climax of all this was his desire to die young, of tuberculosis.

In his devotion to Our Lady there was also some exaggeration. Even at night he would have liked to be awakened every fifteen minutes, when the clock struck the quarter hour, to greet her with a Hail Mary. He wished to pray to her even in his dreams. He would trace her name with the ties of the liturgical vestments. Stopping in Giulianova on the way to Isola del Gran Sasso, the Brother cook saw him jump in the air so he could reach an image of Our Lady to kiss it. When he thought that no one would see him, he would stop to kiss the images of Our Lady that were on the doors and in the corridors. The pictures he had of Our Lord on the Cross were "discolored" because of his kisses. He had devised special arguments in order to get permission to have Mary's name emblazoned on his chest with a burning branding iron, or at least with a pocketknife. To his great regret, permission was never granted.

He became sullen when a carefree fellow student spoke jokingly about Our Lady's ring that was believed to be kept in Perugia.

Even in his aim for union with God he would go beyond the normal limits. He did not want to hear about anything that would not lead his heart and mind to God. But wasn't it necessary to go to God with all kinds of news? Especially with the times in which they were living, wasn't it more important than ever to know what was going on so as to be able to pray about it?

In cases where things were expected but never occurred, he would laugh and say: "See? A waste of time. We were all worried, but nothing happened. It's better just to stick to God." There would be someone who would get tired of him always talking only about good things and they would tell him off.

In his obedience also there was perhaps something a bit fanatical. He would take his director seriously even when he was joking. One time, wanting to be left alone, the director told him to go off and tend to the sheep, and he got ready to go off and do just that: the Passionists had a total of eleven head of livestock, counting lambs, gelded rams and a goat. The director told him to scratch his stomach and he started doing so. He told him to chew his food well because he had digestion problems, and he chewed even those things that did not need to be chewed. The director explained to him that he could not wear the little penitential chain any more because he was weak, and besides he could no longer even keep up the normal penitential practices of the community; at most he could wear the chain over his habit. And so Gabriel went around all day with the chain in full view of everyone, at school, at table, at prayer and at recreation.

To train the students in humility, there was the practice of mistreating them with all kinds of reprimands, even unwarranted ones. The student who was the object of this barrage had to take it all in silence and on his knees, not getting up until he was told to after it was all finished. Once in a while the Superior would forget to tell Gabriel to get up and Gabriel would stay there on his knees while the rest of the day went by, until someone noticed that he was missing and would go get him.

The House rules forbad talking in the corridors, so he took a fellow student all the way to the other side of the House, inside the bell tower, to give him a message from the Superior. When he was sick, he would even ask permission to change his position in bed.

What can we say about the odd ways in which he and the culture of his day expressed their esteem for chastity? Do not look at, do not talk to, do not even think about women or sex. They tried to be angels instead of accepting human nature as it was.

In making judgments today about this kind of behavior, we have to remember that our knowledge of those times is limited to the way of thinking of those who gave us the reports. The fact is that Gabriel was careful to fulfill his commitments to God and the Church, and was true to himself. He avoided occasions that could open the way to thoughts and feelings that would have been unproductive for him and that could have become negative. This interior experience, which was very legitimate in its human content, is in part expressed by Gabriel and in part described by witnesses using perspectives and language that today are not so important.

We have to remember also that it was under the influence of the centenary celebrations in honor of Saint Aloysius Gonzaga, which took place in the Catholic world in the first half of the year 1891, that Gabriel's name was added to the list of those being considered for canonization. The postulator of Gabriel's cause, and many of the witnesses, including his director, were very happy to force Gabriel into the mold of Gonzaga; but, on the other hand, Gonzaga himself is not always believable because of hagiographic distortions. Anyway, the young Passionist seemed like a modern version of the young Jesuit, and there were those who wanted to make him a close copy of Gonzaga.

Other aspects of Gabriel's Religious life, which might seem strange today and not considered a sign of sanctity at all, were a part of the culture of his day, which had its own way of living the ascetic Christian life and of expressing the relationship between the Religious life and the world.

The ascetic life is essential in Religious experience. It is the work necessary for ascending the heights to God and becoming acceptable to him. For the Christian, this is accomplished by imitating Jesus Christ, the unifying feature of whose life was his death on the Cross for the salvation of humanity in obedience to the heavenly Father.

No one is born already completely prepared to follow

Jesus Christ or already having set out on that road. We are born in a nature that has been altered by sin, and instead of being attracted by obedience to God and love of others, we are drawn to take advantage of others and to slink away from God.

The commitment to asceticism helps to regain what tends otherwise to be lost; it is like taking firm hold once again of the reins. It is the means by which human life, little by little, is put back where it was when God created it and when there was no sin. It is a state of complete fulfillment, consisting of loving God and others, without any attachments to worldly interests.

To be able to make this uphill climb — asceticism — it is necessary to be free and unencumbered, not weighed down by ambivalent values that could compete with God, who is the absolute value. In the same way, it would not be possible to climb the Gran Sasso if you were carrying a television and a refrigerator. It is a road that requires a certain amount of struggle, but for a purpose. It has been called "mortification," but it leads to "life" at another level, not to "death" as destruction. Authentic Christianity does not seek mortification in order to eliminate what is part of being human; rather authentic Christianity seeks to subdue what is rebellious, to readjust what is out of kilter, to purify what shows traces of contamination. It is like refining gold in a furnace to be able then to give it as a gift.

The experience of God does not change one's basic psychology. We do not act without hope of gaining some gratification or satisfaction. No one can deprive themselves of something just to dig deeper into emptiness, but only to fill themselves more completely.

Gabriel does not fix his eyes on women. This is not because they are ugly or because they are of the devil: God would never ask that half of the human race be excluded from our love. Gabriel simply did not want the focus of his heart and thoughts to be distracted from Our Lady. One could object that this could also have been accomplished by looking everyone in the face. The choice depends on the culture of the time that produces certain ways of living and on how deeply rooted one's holiness is.

Gabriel was reflective and silent not because it was bad to speak, to have friendships, to hear about what is going on in the world or to go and see the Pope, but because for him it was enough to be with God and, in his prayer, to be present to everyone and to all the things happening in the world.

He did not eat little because it was bad to eat, but because if he had given free rein to his appetite, he would have eaten more than he needed and would have found it difficult to pray, study and grow in his daily dedication.

By working this way, Gabriel kept in check those things in life that tended to go off on their own. Nothing in him fled the lordship of the Lord Jesus, everything was subject to Christ and was progressing in becoming harmoniously conformed to the Lord.

As time passed, Gabriel's impatient eagerness to become like Jesus grew ever stronger and nothing could satisfy it. Jesus was the one whose entire way of life consisted in dying for others, as the Father had willed. Gabriel was a student and could not do a lot for others, he could not even go out and give himself to the poor in priestly ministry. Inside the Passionist House he studied and prepared himself, but he needed concrete actions in which he could soon express the ardor that consumed him. He could not put off till tomorrow the need to make himself like the Crucified Lord. This is why he was always looking for new sacrifices to make. He wanted to give his life for Jesus and for others, and it was sometimes only with difficulty that he would come up with something new.

From this desire there arose behavior that puzzled others and that could not be explained without understanding his heart. Little symbolic actions were no longer enough; he wanted to burn into his body, or at least carve into it with a

pocketknife, the name "Mary." It was not enough to speak
of Our Lady of Sorrows; he wanted to take a vow because he
felt that a vow linked him more tightly to her. And so on.

Gabriel's inner problem was that he had to achieve the
greatest accomplishments with the smallest of things. As he
sought to fill insignificant acts with great meaning —
whether to look at something or not, to speak or not, to touch
or not — he was in danger of going to excesses. The only
experience in which he would feel finally satisfied in his desire to give himself completely would be death. There he
would have the feeling of truly giving everything, and in
Christian hope there he would have the certainty that after
death he would be able to love to his full capacity.

On the other hand, his great estimation of little things
is the secret and example he left for everyone. It is by living
simply that he fully became what he is. Nowadays it is always more difficult to find people capable of being truly satisfied and content with just ordinary things.

To understand his condemnation of the world it is necessary to make a conscious effort to place ourselves in his
culture and to peer deeply into his soul.

Among the various meanings of "world" that are found
in the Bible, there was prevalent for a long time in Christian spirituality the negative and pessimistic meaning: the
world was where the devil was at work, where evil had the
upper hand — after all, it was stronger than good in
humanity's negligible ability to resist it. The ideal choice then
was to flee the world, fight it, hate it.

This was the common perspective in Gabriel's time and
was why he too saw the world as though it were engaged in
constant conspiracy against the Church and against human
attainment of salvation. The model of perfection that he
adopted was that of contempt for the world and opposition
to it; he chose to flee the world, for only with difficulty could
one attain salvation in the world. To his friend Giovannetti
he wrote: "The world is full of obstacles and dangers. It is a

very difficult thing to save the one soul we have, but because of this you mustn't become discouraged if the Lord calls you to live in the world; for even there you can be saved." This last part is added almost as a concession.

But the Bible presents the world also as a place that is loved by God. It was for the whole of mankind, all men and women whom God so loved, that he gave his Son. The Spirit of the Risen Christ is at work in the world. But we will have to wait for the Second Vatican Council to put this concept back into Christian consciousness and experience.

In the world, Christ and the Spirit are also present, it is not just Satan who is here. Earthly realities have positive value in themselves, without it being necessary that the Church assign this value to them. There are possibilities for genuinely living a true Christian life in the world, even to the point of sanctity, and not only possibilities of perdition. Nowadays, the Christian experience of fleeing the world, insofar as evil is present in it, cannot fail to be integrated into the overall experience of being a part of the world, insofar as there is present in it good that must be upheld and developed. But Gabriel lived the values that were his and of his time, and they were enough for him to fully love God and the world in God.

He went on without second thoughts.

Upon watching him arrive at Morrovalle, one of his colleagues wondered with puzzlement: "Will this fancy dancer make it?" Later, as an old man, thinking about him again and writing one of the best accounts of Gabriel's life, this same confrere would say: quite often when I think of him "tears come to my eyes and I am filled with shame for having been so far from the virtues that he attained in such a short time."

This colleague was Bernard Silvestrelli. He would be Superior General of the Passionists for twenty-five years and would live until the year 1911. In 1988 he joined the former "fashion plate" on the altar of beatified sainthood.

Chapter Sixteen

Not Everything Goes Smoothly

It may seem that it was just too easy for him: the results may have been considerable, but what effort was necessary when difficulties seemed to magically disappear and everyone was eager to take their hat off to him saying what a good job he had done? The temptations of the flesh were simply not there; his heart was flying straight as an arrow toward God, untouched by the youthful confusion of a normal person. His instincts and passions were like the surface of a calm sea. The devil had no power over him; perhaps the devil was there snarling at him, but he was unable to snatch him from Our Lady's loving embrace.

But this was not the case with Gabriel; he had the same difficulties as everyone else, plus some more.

Community life in a Religious House is not a simple cross to bear; it can be as difficult as living at home with one's family. This was true for Gabriel, even though he was already used to life in community, having grown up as one of as many as ten children. Making accommodations for others was a never-ending job, and each person can also be a problem for every other person. You could not be connected to everyone in the same way, and there was always a possible disagreement brewing with the others.

In his relationships with the other members of the community, Gabriel was refined and respectful, but he could cause difficulties for some people. The sneers would fly like arrows: "Shut up!"; "Here is the advocate of lost causes"; "Put a sock in it, you holy-Joe"; "Don't be such a pain"; and these comments would be accompanied by gestures even more eloquent than the words. It seemed that there was even someone who tried to slap him in the face; we do not know if the slap was blocked or if it was actually given. The story of the slap has circulated in the Passionist community for a long time. It was attempted by Gabriel's fellow student Francis Xavier del Principe, who later became Provincial and then Superior General and had Gabriel's cause for beatification introduced.

Gabriel just barely avoided another smack, this time with Father Anthony Pacini, the Pastor of Ornano Grande, who was often a guest in the Passionist House. Even priests sometimes lose their patience. Father Pacini was a clergyman with pro-Bourbonist leanings; he was hot-tempered and had been four times imprisoned for his hostility toward the new Piedmontese regime. He came across Gabriel in the silent corridors of the House and greeted him loudly. Gabriel lowered his head, smiled, and continued on his way without responding. Father Pacini thought he was being rude, "and since I have a short temper, I was tempted to give him a slap." But another Passionist later explained to him that Gabriel did not speak in places set aside for silence or at times when silence was to be observed.

Relationships with those in authority can be another difficulty in community life. Gabriel would accept authority without showing any contrary reactions, but knowing his independent nature, it could not have been easy for him. Those in authority would make him restrain himself in his Marian devotion and in his dreams of heroic mortification. Norbert would also give him a hard time by sometimes treating him rudely in order to build up his character. He too would publicly call him a holy-Joe, a nosey-body, or a skew-nose, referring to the crooked slant of his nose. He did not spare him the feigned reprimands that all the students had to endure while on their knees; these would be seen as humorous today, but then they were quite stinging. Norbert was tough with him, would show him disdain and put him down.

In the task of perfecting the tendencies of Gabriel's character and temperament, behavior modification was achieved, but only as a result of hard work. For example, as concerns his propensity to get angry, Norbert said it was changed into "patience, acceptance, meekness." But up till the end, one could see how difficult this was for him: "Once in a while anger would boil up in his soul and you could even see the external signs." But he did not give in to it. Even in his final illness, his director noted how hard he worked at repressing his anger, and feared that he would yield to his rage right at the end. Gabriel quickly sensed his fear and told him: "Don't worry, Father, I won't grow impatient."

It was not true that the devil sat doing nothing while Gabriel made his ascent. We know of "terrible and prolonged temptations" against faith, "especially while he was praying." Evil knows that prayer is the reinforced concrete used to build holiness: it can withstand anything. At certain times, therefore, the evil one would launch every possible attack to make him skip his prayer or at least to make him remiss in it; it put into his head "the most horrid vileness" about the subject that he wanted to meditate upon. At these times, "going to pray was like going into battle with temptation."

There was a period in which he was "assaulted by such terrible ideas against God and urged to pronounce such vehement blasphemies that he would actually be completely exhausted from the struggle." Sometimes he would go to his director to ask for help and would arrive "looking as if he were possessed." He faced "temptations that were sometimes exceedingly strong and terrible," explained Norbert who knew everything about him and who knew that it was not true that Gabriel did everything "by virtue of giftedness and enthusiasm, spurred on by the consolations and desires given by the Holy Spirit."

The greater threat to the virtue of hope came from the temptation of presumption and not from the temptation to lack trust. Presumption was a more insidious temptation and would attack him even on his death bed.

The trials that he was subjected to did not have any respect even for the most intimate and tender experience that was his: his devotion to Our Lady. Norbert writes: "It was a frightening thing, the furor with which the devil assailed him" in this area, especially in his final days. "Like a choking noose about his neck, Satan tried to do him violence and to throw him against the very object of his love." It assaulted him "by stirring up in his mind such horrendous insults, abuse, revulsion and blasphemies that the poor young man couldn't take it any more." But the Lord allowed at least a little bit of peace, as a final favor, because "the final assault" ended "a few months before his death."

In Gabriel's day, hagiographic writings were discreetly silent about the struggles for the virtue of purity, struggles whose principal cause was not always the temptations sent by the devil. Special gifts of God cannot be excluded in this area, but they should not be necessarily admitted, just to please cultural expectations. As far as Gabriel is concerned, we know that the virtue of purity was put to the test when he was just a step away from death. His life had included the normal path of integration of youthful sexuality into the experience of God. His path included natural ups and downs and the snares set by the devil. Besides this, he had to deal with tuberculosis, which affects sexuality.

What effect would his romantic feelings for a young girl of Spoleto have had on his inner being? It is absurd to assume that such a relationship would have left no mark. But even these feelings that could have possibly made him a husband ended up being drawn into the vortex of the love that bound him to the Crucified Lord and to Our Lady of Sorrows. Writing to his father from Isola del Gran Sasso on December 27, 1860, and responding to the complaint that he did not write frequently enough, Gabriel explained that he had written "three other letters," two of which were addressed to his father and the third of which "was addressed to Mrs. Mary Masi." This was the grandmother of Mary Pennacchietti, the girl who was the focus of Gabriel's attentions in Spoleto. Perhaps she had already gotten married; however, nothing can be inferred from what he said in his letter. But knowing Gabriel's habit of sending greetings, offering advice and asking pardon of everyone in his letters, it would not be out of place if the missing or withheld letter had contained some special words for her.

Among Gabriel's different trials, we did not speak about what happened when it was God himself who was the direct agent of thorough and exhaustive testing, something to which he sometimes subjects those who seek nothing but him. Gabriel was not exempt from this testing; he was "tormented by aridity of spirit, by darkness, by repulsion": even dark nights of the soul, the supreme purification, the ultimate test of faithfulness, when you do not know any more whether God loves you still or whether he exists.

The Gabriel who was all sweetness and niceness just did not exist. However fragile and gentle he might have been, he went through all the hard knocks of life, both as a layman and as a Passionist, and in all of them he came out all right. He was a fighter who would be victorious right up to the final bout of the challenge.

The definitive proof of this would be the physical decline he would suffer while he was still a young man: he realized that he would die when he was only twenty-four years old and did not even bat an eye; he was on the verge of welcoming that future in which his dream of becoming a priest was within arm's reach, but he had to watch his plans disappear and had to prepare instead to leave this world. He had asked to depart and desired to leave because he would then be able to finally satisfy his longing to be consumed as a sacrifice and a gift. But he remained human through and through, and welcoming death was the ultimate penance and the supreme purification that any human creature could undergo.

Chapter Seventeen

Firmly Grounded in History

His wet nurse in Petrignano, his mother, his father, his family, especially his sister Mary Louisa, the family governess Pacifica, the various tutors who came to the Possenti home; the Brothers of the Christian Schools, the Servites, the Oratorians, the Jesuits, the Passionists; ancient and modern culture, society, the political situation, spirituality, the Church: who can say which influences and hidden forces had come together to shape his personality? Even saints come from a specific history and are part of a particular history. God has set them apart so that they can say something to history. Gabriel was born of a particular people and he lived in a way that was meaningful for his people.

He absorbed much from his family, where the current political problems made their presence felt and even caused injury, where the spiritual life was nourished not only by devotional practices but also by doctrinal writings such as those of Saint Francis de Sales and Saint Alphonsus Liguori.

At school he learned the different ideas of the time and its culture. He worked at his own Christian formation, welcoming what was given and giving himself wholly to the projects that allowed him to experience in practice what was being taught in theory. The Sodality of Mary and the other Confraternities trained him in bearing witness and helped him to grow in conviction, as today's Church groups do for young people.

The Jesuits taught him discipline, precision, the correct use of the will, discernment, the proper worth of human talents, and asceticism as the foundation for truly following God. With the Passionists he learned to be flexible and expressive, to give space to his feelings; he realized that he was capable of putting his whole heart into whatever work he was doing. The founder of the Passionists, Saint Paul of the Cross, did not have rigid structures for prayer or for spiritual direction; rather he allowed the creativity of the Spirit to play its role in the preparation of his spiritual sons. It was as a Passionist that Gabriel found the climax and completion of the journey for which he had been destined.

It is appropriate to say a word here about Gabriel's relationship with history and the unfolding of the political and social events of his day.

The brief span of his twenty-four years coincided with the momentous period of the Italian Risorgimento. Up until 1848, the ideals of democracy, independence, national unity, and the vindication of civil rights, were sought by semi-terroristic bands, but these were easily suppressed by the ruling powers in the different Italian states. In the beginning secret societies, then intellectual theoreticians and individuals able to put theories into practice, succeeded in fostering the proliferation of localized libertarian movements, which were very useful in spreading the ideals of the Risorgimento and in raising awareness of them. Insurrections would rise up like sparks leaping from a fire; they would occur from Piedmont to Sicily, passing through Modena, Bologna, Macerata, Teramo, Naples and finally coming together in the wars for independence.

In the first part of 1848, the more sensible governing authorities granted democratic constitutions for their territories: Pius IX for the Papal States, Ferdinand II of the Bourbons for the Kingdom of Naples, and Charles Albert of Savoy for the Kingdom of Piedmont. But the momentum for the ideal of national unity did not abate. The attempt to unite the nation according to a kind of neo-Guelph plan, that is, a federation of States under the authority of the Pope, was unsuccessful. This plan, conceived by Vincent Gioberti and Anthony Rosmini, failed in the same year, 1848, and saw the people confused by an avalanche of events that they found difficult to understand: the granting and then the repeal of different democratic constitutions; the first war of independence, which ended with the defeat of the Piedmontese army and Pius IX ordering the papal army to stop at the Austrian border because of the danger of schism; the exile of Charles Albert of Savoy; the assassination of the Prime Minister of the Papal Government, Pellegrino Rossi, at the hand of Ciceruacchio; the Pope fleeing to Gaeta; and the proclamation of the Roman Republic headed by Armellini, Saffi and Mazzini.

Gabriel, a ten-year-old boy in Spoleto at this time, could not have realized all that was going on; he would have only been aware of the death of his brother Paul, somehow involved in all of what was happening.

Gabriel's father was certainly loyal to the sovereignty of the Pope; he was after all an official in the Spoleto papal delegation. In his own family and among the circle of noble and well-to-do families, there was concern for defending proper spiritual values, which were believed to be guaranteed only if the Church maintained its influence.

The years 1850 through 1856 were the time of Francis' schooling with the Jesuits and were peaceful years for the Papal States; Pius IX had once more taken charge and was trying to make his rule more popular with the people.

Afterward, the fighting for Italian unity continued, although the Papal States would still survive for a long time; but Gabriel was much more interested in other struggles. However, when he left the Papal States on July 8, 1859 to go to Isola del Gran Sasso, he found himself immersed in the confrontational climate of the road that led to Italian unity. This had notable effects on his life.

The people of Abruzzi were happy with their sovereign, Ferdinand II of Naples, and were in no hurry to shake themselves free of his yoke. But the Carbonaro contagion, that is, the clandestine work of secret associations that sought liberal reforms in Italian society, had already widely spread, and patriotic fervor for unity was being quickly transmitted, even by the clergy.

In the first part of September, 1860, the news that Garibaldi had entered Naples reached Teramo. On October 15th, Victor Emmanuel II crossed the Tronto River. In Giulianova he was greeted with widespread rejoicing and with the singing of the *Te Deum* in the churches.

No sooner had the new rulers taken over than taxes were increased and the cost of living went up so much that the people of Abruzzi, already in difficulty because of the year's poor harvest, went into sudden and furious revolt. They were given military support by the garrison of the Kingdom, which was still stationed at the Fort of Civitella on the River Tronto. The Piedmontese reaction to this revolt did not even leave breathing room. In December, General Pinelli led the army and in fifteen days subdued every foolish ambition of rebellion; he sowed terror with firing squads and hangings. Pinelli is famous still today for his cruelty, his northern racism, and his Masonic anticlericalism. His excesses were unappealing even to his superiors, who recalled him to Torino.

On March 20th, the army also managed to deceitfully destroy the Fort of Civitella on the River Tronto after a heavy bombardment; the exploding of the artillery fire ran up the sides of the mountains and echoed off the face of the Gran Sasso, causing great concern in Gabriel's community. On the morning of March 18th, the Piedmontese "gave themselves ruthlessly to the attack with continuous bombardments for two consecutive days and nights, such that even the snakes were terrified."

In June and July a new uprising directly involved the countryside of the province of Teramo around Isola del Gran Sasso: Fano Adriano, Tossicia, and Castelli. Although this insurrection was less violent, it was put down with bloodshed just like the preceding revolts, this time under the leadership of General Gualtieri. Once again there were merciless executions, some of which were carried out right in front of the Passionist House, in order to dissuade the Religious from harboring rebels. Gualtieri also was recalled because of excesses in putting down the rebellions. He had even published a decree that condemned to the firing squad "anyone who gives shelter to a brigand."

Nor were members of the clergy who had anti-Savoy leanings, including Bishops, exempt from arrest, exile, and even some executions by firing squad. Religious Houses suspected of hiding revolutionaries were searched.

Speaking of this period, the terms "brigand" and "brigandage" were also applied to the supporters of the House of the Bourbons, but incorrectly so. The phenomenon of brigandage must be distinguished from reactions to the Piedmontese occupation, which were of a popular character and which targeted the wealthy residents who opportunistically allied themselves with the new rulers, giving no opposition at all.

On February 17, 1861, the Piedmontese decree suppressing all Religious Institutes was published; however, the rigor with which it was applied varied from place to place. In Abruzzi, it would not go into full effect until 1866, but already in 1861 clerics were prevented from receiving the major orders of subdiaconate, diaconate, and priesthood. This was the period in which Gabriel, now at the end of his theological studies, would have been admitted to major orders. His community, already condemned to extinction, was not allowed to ordain new priests. Because of this, the students of Isola del Gran Sasso would be taken to the Marches the following year so that they could be ordained.

On January 26, 1860, Norbert wrote to Sante Possenti: "I hope that in another year Gabriel will celebrate Mass." On February 5, 1861: "Gabriel is well. If things improve, I hope that he will be ordained in the autumn, and perhaps even this Christmas he will celebrate his first Mass." And on May 9th of the same year: "If the time is right, his ordination will take place without delay. And if a change comes about soon, I can almost promise you that he will sing his first Mass around Christmas." That would have been the Christmas when Gabriel, already stricken by his first serious bout with tuberculosis, was not even able to leave his room to go to Midnight Mass.

Gabriel himself, writing on December 19th to his father and on December 30th to his brother Michael, would say: "At this time, I would have perhaps already been a priest had it not been for the lack of ordaining prelates that prevented me from being ordained. But that is what God has wanted, and it is what I want too." This was his farewell to the dream that had captivated him from his youth.

His brother Henry would later testify that Gabriel was never ordained a priest "because of the difficulties of the times."

In all of these explanations there is a bit of truth: there was a shortage of Bishops who could confer Holy Orders, because they were prohibited from doing so; the roads were insecure, but they were not necessarily prohibitive; Gabriel did get sick, but his illness became serious only in December. The whole truth is that Gabriel did not become a priest because of the political situation in which he was embroiled and which, from September of 1861 on, prevented the conferring of Holy Orders. Otherwise he would have been ordained subdeacon and deacon by October or November, and would probably have been ordained a priest in December.

Priesthood was not necessary for him to arrive at the fullness of his potential, but, psychologically, would have been the greatest moment of his life and, emotionally, the joy-filled high point.

This then was how he took part in the history that surrounded him and how he was affected by it. Young people of his age also participated in this same history, but they did so by aligning themselves with the different factions and feeding on the various ideologies; in contrast, Gabriel's participation took the form of contemplating the Crucified Lord and loving his contemporaries from the perspective of Christ the Savior.

If he had remained in Spoleto, he too could have found himself involved in some battle for the unity of Italy, or he could have remained silently loyal up to the end to the government that had given him his bread and butter. But he did not feel it in himself to live in such a situation of contradiction, which in the name of new priorities was sweeping aside other values. The direction that history was taking did not appeal to him; he didn't find himself at ease in it; it was not for him. God called him to die in that period of history in another way. His death was mysteriously connected with the history of his time. Dying without reaching his dream of the priesthood was his way of paying the painful price for the unity of Italy. In this, he was like so many young people who, in every age, die in battle for their people without ever bringing to completion their noble and significant plans for the future.

This was the history that intruded on his life and made itself felt so deeply: not only because his letters were intercepted, or because he was prevented from returning to the Marches, or because the road to priesthood was closed to him; but also because it enabled him to experience self-abandonment to God in times of danger, because it led him to understand the pain of the oppressed and of the "brigands" who sought refuge in the Passionist House, because it made him reflect on the intensity of the passions for unity and of patriotism, because it provided him with the opportunity to experience in God the human condition that he shared with everyone else.

Firmly grounded in his history, in less than six years his adventure in holiness was completed.

Chapter Eighteen

A Celebrated Death

Why did he die at twenty-four years of age? That was his destiny; it could have been because of the austere life he lived or because of his fragile health or simply because he overdid it.

The scientific cause of death was pulmonary tuberculosis brought on by the Koch bacillus, which was common enough at the time and usually untreatable.

From the moment of Gabriel's death, Norbert did everything he could to eliminate the impression that his death had been the result of the Passionists' severe life-style. Nor did he accept the theory that Gabriel had contracted the disease because of his "weak constitution" or that it had been part of his hereditary make-up. He came up with the convincing hypothesis that the sickness could be traced back to the "abuses that he subjected himself to in his younger days," such as the exhausting hunting expeditions he would go on, especially in autumn, that would cause him to sweat in the damp cool of the woods, where he would sometimes fall, and during which he did not eat regularly. He explained once again that after joining the Passionists, Gabriel put on weight, improved in color, and enjoyed "very good health for nearly four years, maybe even more."

The reality, however, was that Francis Possenti's physical condition had always been fragile, and this was the indirect cause of his taking ill. His physical characteristics were those typical of energetic long-limbed individuals, that is, he was slender and slim with quick movements and decisive actions, which corresponded to his being strong-willed with an active temperament. In him, however, this physical framework was present in a person who suffered from respiratory difficulties. He would easily get sore throats, which was one of the reasons his father showed astonishment at his determination to join the Passionists.

As a Passionist he found a life-style that was not easy with regard to looking after his health. He himself would often say, obviously referring to the way of life in the Passionist House: "If we were always concerned about our health, we would never do anything." He was very impassioned in his commitment to the spiritual life, and all the young students were so overcome by enthusiasm that they would neglect paying attention to material concerns, including their own physical well-being. The spiritual directors had a difficult task in restraining the fervor of the novices and students, at least making them avoid excesses in penitential practices; but oftentimes they themselves led heroic lives in this very regard. Moreover, community life and the sharing of living space and of linens could only contribute to the possibility of spreading disease, which during those years took the lives of other young members of the Passionist family. Gabriel had found the spiritual environment suited to his determination to quickly become a saint and he threw himself into it completely without the slightest concern for anything else.

A year after he had joined the Passionists, his sister Teresa met him at Fermo and found him "in a deplorable state." "It seemed that the religious habit weighed him down and that he could barely support it."

The following year, more or less, in September of 1858, his brother Michael met him at Pievetorina and found him happy "but pale and a bit worn out." In saying good-bye to him, he went away with a "bad feeling." Still at Pievetorina, a student of the Franciscan Third Order, Angelo de Mattia, who was making a spiritual retreat in the Passionist House, saw him looking very pale and asked the director if he were sick. "He's not been well for some time," responded the director, "and there is little hope of being able to do anything for him." If he was already at death's doorstep just two years after joining the Passionists, it is difficult to understand how Norbert could claim that he enjoyed good health for more than four years.

Rather, with his sister Teresa and his brother Michael, we can maintain that the first symptoms of Gabriel's sickness were already visible, at least to the knowing eyes of his family, after just one year in the Passionist House. However, this was not evident to the eyes of the less experienced Superiors; otherwise they would have sent him back to his family, as they had done with his Spoleto colleague and novice companion Caesar Calandrelli, who had been sent back home because it was suspected that he was suffering from a bad form of pulmonary tuberculosis.

In Gabriel's case, we do not know when the doctors started to speak of the possibility of tuberculosis, or of tuberculosis that was already well advanced. As soon as this diagnosis was made, however, Norbert relieved him of many of the duties which he would normally have had to fulfill as part of community life; he also informed the Provincial Superior of this decision.

In his final year, Gabriel's behavior clearly showed that he himself felt that death was now near. This inner knowledge of death approaching soon may have been communicated to him by God, or he may have become aware of it from his ebbing strength. He just seemed too much like someone who was slowly closing himself to everyone and who would concentrate on one thing only. The other members of the community saw that he was making incredible spiritual progress. "You'd have to have been blind" not to notice. "In that final year he was soaring." From the determined way in which he was living, it could be felt in the air that he would soon die.

Norbert struggled with how to properly direct his spiritual life in this final period. Even in the area of spiritual direction, a disciple who is just too good can be a source of embarrassment for his master. One morning Norbert left his room lost in thought as to how to address this situation, and his eyes happened to go to the window looking out on the courtyard. He saw that the first winter snow had fallen, and that growing in the snow was a beautiful lily! He rubbed his eyes, looked again, and no longer saw the lily. He took this as a sign from heaven that the decisions he was making and the method he was using were correct.

The situation went downhill in December of 1861. Gabriel's chronic, dry cough, that had seemed no more than a winter cold, grew into a full-blown serious hemoptysis that brought up a lot of blood. There was no doubt: the tuberculosis had arrived at the final stage, his lungs were being ripped apart, death was knocking at the door. Gabriel realized what was going on and experienced a slight wooziness, somewhere between joy and fear. Then suddenly, as if he had received formal word of the announcement that he was expecting, he ran to the tabernacle holding tight the handkerchief that he had used to wipe up the blood he had coughed up onto his chest. A whisper sealed and completed the pact that had been made some time ago: Jesus, blood for blood, love for love, life for life.

His death was simply the culmination of the celebration: the definitive offering of his life.

On December 19th he wrote to his father to wish him a Merry Christmas. The chief sentiment he expressed was gratitude to Our Lady for having removed him from the situation in the world. On Christmas, they did not make him go down into the chapel for Midnight Mass, but he took part in it from the little window in the choir.

On the 30th he sent his last letter; it was to his brother Michael, who had sent him Christmas greetings. "With his heart in his pen," he gave advice for proper living. "Do you want to love? Love Mary. People on this earth cannot make you happy. The drama of this world passes quickly. Farewell, dear brother. Do as I have recommended, it is a matter of eternal happiness."

This was his farewell not only to his brother but to life as well. There was a feeling of maturity and fulfillment. His peace was in the will of God, for which he felt such attraction that he could not escape it. His plans of priesthood went up in smoke, but it did not even occur to him to say: Well, maybe next time. What did it matter? The only thing that mattered was the will of God. Now his life consisted more in God than it did in breathing air. He was ready. He had bet everything in order to win everything in faith.

As long as he was still able, he continued to go out into the garden to get a breath of fresh air, especially when a bright ray of winter sunlight would appear and reveal life's smile. On such occasions, Xavier Tortella, a simple countryboy who took care of the sheep of the Passionist House, would come running over to him to chat, very happy when he saw him. From these "chats" we have other items of testimony: Gabriel told Xavier that he was to say the Hail Mary many times every day. Xavier objected, saying that he already said about fifty every day. Gabriel then put a medal around his neck and smiling said: "Say one every time you look at this." The next day he waited for him as if awaiting someone returning from a mission: "How did the Hail Marys go?" "I didn't do anything else but say Hail Marys, because the medal was always before my eyes!" "Good, keep on doing just that."

Eventually mere walking became exhausting. His gait was unstable. To make sure that he didn't fall, someone accompanied him when he went on his walks. People observed that when he went to Communion one of his confreres would hold him up.

On Sunday, February 16, 1862, he attended two Masses and received Holy Communion, but it was clear that he could no longer keep himself on his feet. He was ordered to bed.

On Monday the seventeenth, the director went to his

room and found him "on his feet and coughing up mouthfuls of blood." This was the second hemoptysis. Nothing could be done. The doctor who had come to see him wanted to stay with him through the night. Norbert made himself strong and explained to Gabriel that the situation was serious. The word "death" was used. This was nothing new for Gabriel, but he did go through a brief moment of sadness, like the painful shudder of the end. "Not even a minute, but just a very brief instant," Norbert was careful to specify. But after all, Gabriel was still quite young.

When the Viaticum arrived, he had to be forced by obedience to remain in bed, for he wanted to prostrate himself on the ground and give expression to the gratitude and love that blazed inside of him. As was the Passionist custom, the community was present and the sick Gabriel begged forgiveness for the annoyance and poor example that he had given, and he entrusted himself to their prayer. As he spoke, they were all moved to tears. In the silence of his thanksgiving, they could hear him whisper: "May the most holy, the most lovely, the most adorable will of God always be done."

He was ready for death, and this readiness soon turned into impatience; now that he felt prepared, he could not wait to die. After receiving Holy Viaticum, he wanted to die with that blessed feeling. Wednesday the 19th came, and he hoped that Saint Joseph would carry him off on the day dedicated to him. Saturday the 22nd arrived, and he longed for Our Lady to come and take him on her day, but nothing happened. Norbert tried to keep him calm by having him reflect on the need to be as well prepared as possible.

Sunday the 23rd was the day of Holy Communion, and so he spent it immersed in the Lord's presence in a very special way. Not even in danger of death could you receive Holy Communion every day.

While Gabriel lost count of the days and the members of the community vied for turns at being by the bedside of their sick confrere, there took place precious scenes of a drama that no one wanted to miss because of how touching it was; witnesses have handed these scenes on to us in the richness of their every detail. Some of these moments, Norbert said, were things that "would move even a rock to tears."

With the excuse of avoiding the temptation to pride, Gabriel convinced the director to destroy a little notebook in which he had kept track of the different graces received from Our Lady. "Like a blockhead I ran off to get the notebook. I was sorry then that I did so and I'm sorry still," Norbert would later lament. But that record has been swallowed by the flames of the kitchen hearth, and the most intimate secrets of Gabriel's soul can no longer be known with certainty.

The ailing Gabriel was thinking also about his father in Spoleto, whom he had promised to inform if his health should deteriorate in the future. "Was it time to let him know?" he asked Norbert. Norbert gently reassured him: "I'll take care of it," he said. But he did so only after Gabriel's death.

Vincent Tranquilli, from Gerano in Rome, wanted to be assigned to tend to Gabriel during the night shifts, so as to have an example from the dying young man. One night he asked Gabriel to pray to the Lord for him, so that he might be healed of an affliction. Gabriel agreed to do so, but after a bit said to him: "You know that thing you asked me about? Well, it's not God's will. It's a cross that God wants you to carry with you until you die." It was a very bad hernia which, in fact, Vincent would always have.

Gabriel was grateful to those who came to be with him and never stopped expressing his thanks. In his presence, the doctor was also moved to the point of tears and had to turn his head aside. Every once in a while Gabriel would remember someone else from whom he had received something, like the shepherd boy who had brought him milk, and would ask someone to thank these people for him.

To his companions who came one after the other to tend to his needs he would suggest once in a while that they go get some sleep or take something to eat or have a snuff of tobacco, a common practice in those days. "I wouldn't want you to get sick because of me," he said to one. And to another: "What can I do for you who have done so much for me?" After one of his companions had been with him for a long time, he implored the director to send the companion off so he could get a bit of good wine for himself; he did not realize that it was not the right time of the day. The companion had to pretend to go off and drink some wine in order to put Gabriel at peace.

He did not miss a thing, not even Norbert's pain when he would grow sad at the thought of having to lose his "dear little son." Gabriel would smile at him in silence and hold his hand tight.

When he remained in bed because of his illness, no one was able to get him to take off the Passionist habit, but at the end he was ordered to remove it, because it was impossible for him to get any rest due to his weak state and the burning fever. While he was taking it off, he wept over it, caressed it, kissed it, and spoke to it, asking pardon for removing it from him.

He spent much time in the company of his great loves of all time. They were all there: the Crucified Lord, Our Lady of Sorrows, the Founder of the Passionists Saint Paul of the Cross, and his other favorite saints. He would speak with them and send warm greetings to the Blessed Sacrament. Even in moments of delirium, which grew more and more frequent, he would dream that he was saying the rosary, or the litanies, or attending Benediction. He asked all who attended him to help him to pray, because by himself he could no longer do it. He also asked them for wholesome thoughts and to read passages from *The Glories of Mary* for him.

He spoke of death with self-assurance, as though he were speaking of a celebration. He would greet people, offer suggestions and make promises. To those who asked him to prepare a little place for them in heaven, he would respond: "I hope to, with the mercy of God and the intercession of my dear Mother." He wanted to make use of all the absolutions and indulgences connected with the different confraternities in which he was enrolled and was happy to receive Extreme Unction, now called the sacrament of the Anointing of the Sick.

The evening of the 26th, it was more difficult than usual for Norbert to leave Gabriel's room. Gabriel himself, always careful to invite him to go and rest, did not say anything this time; indeed, he seemed content to have him remain. Throughout all these days, Norbert was constantly at Gabriel's side so as not to leave him even for a moment without the spiritual support that he needed. You could never be too sure; an angel like Gabriel on the verge of death could cause such great malice on the part of that spoiler of innocence, who is the devil. Back in his own room, Norbert tried to sleep, but was not able to do so even for a moment. The first hours of the night went by and nothing happened. But then the sound of Gabriel's groaning, having now grown agonizing, reached Norbert's room. He jumped from his bed and ran to Gabriel. He heard Gabriel repeating, full of anguish, "My sole merit lies in your wounds!" He understood, and received confirmation from Gabriel, that thoughts of pride and presumption were trying to make their way into Gabriel's being: the temptation to save himself on his own, on his own merit.

After a little while, he grew perturbed again. He tried to turn his head aside and asked: "How did the women get in here? Mary, dear Mother of mine...." An attack on his clear and pure thoughts. Images that tried to contaminate his world where everything was in its proper place, with God at the center. Were these dormant feelings that were emerging from his subconscious in moments of delirium, or true and proper temptations to impurity? Who can say to what level evil could descend in order to try and seize prey that was getting away? Norbert gave him reassurance by suggesting wholesome thoughts and sprinkling holy water.

After these two tense moments, Gabriel became serene and was smiling once more, like he used to do in his best moments. This was how he spent the last three or four hours.

He requested sacramental absolution for the umpteenth time and centered himself once more on the Lord. He felt his life slipping away. There was no longer any breath left in his debilitated lungs. But he was never more aware, and like a movie-director he set the stage for his own death.

It was the morning of February 27th and the first light of morning, reflected off the face of the Gran Sasso, struck the windows of the Passionist House. The community, already up for morning prayer, was called together in Gabriel's room and followed in prayer the progress of his death at dawn. Gabriel held to his heart the image of the Crucified Lord with Our Lady of Sorrows and prayed: "Dear Mother of mine, come quickly." Always in a hurry, this dear blessed son. He pressed the image ever harder against his heart, almost violently, as if he wanted to make it enter his flesh. This was also the result of the instinct to stimulate the heart, whose beating was growing ever weaker, and the lungs, which were hardly functioning. He repeated the invocation of the dying up to "Jesus, Joseph and Mary, let my soul expire in peace with you"; he stretched out the syllables of the word "expire," making it "ex...pi...re," and finished the phrase in a soft exhalation while on his face there was the smile of the ecstasy that carried him off. His face became luminous, suffused with a smile, and then tilted off toward the wall to the left.

He breathed no more. He looked as though he were asleep.

Had Our Lady come to take him away? Those who were present at the moment of death thought so, and it seems legitimate to think that indeed she had. Or it could have been paradise opening itself wide before the soul and casting a reflection on the body that now lay lifeless. In any event, it was a death "without agony, a sweet sleep, indeed a sweet ecstasy, a true rapture."

It was the Thursday before Ash Wednesday, February 27, 1862, around seven o'clock in the morning; the sun had just peeked out above the horizon.

Chapter Nineteen

The Young Man and His Heart

A speeding rocket in the skies of sanctity. Sailing past others and soaring so high that he could not be held back. "He was with us only a few years, and he surpassed us all," Norbert wrote to Sante a month after Gabriel's death.

Everyone felt the same. He was still fresh in the grave yet no one doubted that he would become famous. While he was still alive, whispers circulated that God would exalt him. It was an aura he exuded, a feeling he induced; in fact, no sooner was he dead than there was a race to get "some memento: hair, clothing, writings or something else."

Is this what death is?

That very day, the Superior of the community wrote in the register of the deceased that he lacked no virtue; and, only so as to comply with what was required by the Passionist rules, prayers were offered for the repose of his soul.

The Superior gave conferences to the community on Thursdays and Sundays; the first one after Gabriel's death, he spoke about Gabriel's virtues. Those who went off on preaching missions recounted the story of his death and the people were greatly moved, so much so that they would spontaneously go to confession.

A month later, Norbert wrote a second time to Sante; he wrote to console both Sante and himself. He said that only in faith could he accept this trial; he had felt so utterly destroyed by losing Gabriel that he feared he too would die. But he was convinced that Gabriel was in heaven, and that they needed to pray to him to receive assistance in their difficulties.

Two months later, the first systematic biography had already been prepared. Norbert had written it for Sante Possenti and had entitled it *Summary of the Life and Virtues of Gabriel*; he revised it when Gabriel's cause of canonization was introduced. This biographical *Summary* formed much of the basis of what would later be said about Gabriel. It is a work worthy to be put next to other biographies written by holy directors about their holy directees. In sending it to Sante, Norbert wrote that for the Passionists, Gabriel was like Aloysius Gonzaga or John Berchmans.

In the summer of that same year, 1862, Norbert returned to the Marches with the students. They stopped in Pievetorina and then in Recanati, as had been planned for some time. The event of Gabriel's life and death receded somewhat into the background, but it did not disappear.

In 1866, the decree suspending all Religious communities was enforced against the Passionist community of Isola del Gran Sasso, and so they moved to Manduria, in the province of Taranto.

In 1868, a book on *The Life and Virtues of Francis Possenti: Gabriel of Our Lady of Sorrows* was put out by the Marietti Publishing House of Torino. It was written by Gabriel's classmate, Paul Bonaccia, who had become a priest and was a professor at the seminary in Spoleto. This was the first printed biography to appear and also made great use of Norbert's *Summary*.

In the meantime Gabriel himself did something to make sure that he would not be forgotten. A couple of years after his death, he appeared to his brother Vincent, reprimanding him for his card playing. But since he knew that Vincent's economic situation was difficult, Gabriel gave him three lottery numbers that won Vincent ten thousand lire.

In 1871, his father Sante was dying from a stroke. Father Henry had him touch the image that Gabriel had held to his heart as he was dying, and Sante's affliction left him. Norbert would later recognize that "his first true miracle was the one he worked for his father."

In 1879, Bernard Silvestrelli had the artist Francis Grandi paint a portrait of Gabriel and hung it in the Passionist students' hall at the Scala Santa in Rome. In 1885, he wrote a new biography that he included in a series of writings that was intended to provide positive examples especially to young people.

At this time, Bernard was the Congregation's Superior General, and Norbert was the Superior of the Province of Pietà. Both men were convinced of Gabriel's sanctity, but they were not in favor of introducing causes of canonization for Passionists, as they felt that only the founder of the Passionists should have this honor. They would say that it was important to be a saint, not to be officially recognized as such by the Church. Besides, causes for canonization were an excessive financial burden on the meager resources of the Congregation, which was involved in reopening and rebuilding Houses now that the period of suppression had passed.

In 1891, Father Francis Xavier del Principe was Superior General; he too had been in the novitiate with Gabriel. In preparing the list of Passionists who were appropriate candidates to receive official canonized status in the Church as saints, he included Gabriel's name and ordered the postulator, Father German Ruoppolo, to give him precedence.

In 1892, the postulator went to the Passionist House in Isola del Gran Sasso, still abandoned after the community's departure, to exhume Gabriel's body. By order of the Superiors, he was going to have it transferred to the larger and more easily accessible Passionist House of Our Lady of the Star in Umbria between Assisi and Spoleto. He made the trip incognito, not dressed in the Passionist habit, but he was recognized while still six miles from Isola and was greeted as a hero. The message sent secretly to the local authorities had become a great news item.

On October 17th and 18th, the exhumation took place under the watchful surveillance of the people who did not want to even hear of Gabriel's body being taken elsewhere. The church and the area around the House, together with all the access roads, were patrolled for several days until the people, who in all the outlying areas were of one mind on this issue, realized that the body had remained the whole time in the church, although in a different place. Seeing the people's determination in this matter from the beginning till now, Father German sent a telegram to Rome stating that it was impossible and imprudent to transfer the body elsewhere.

An unexpected occurrence took place and was immediately interpreted as confirmation from on high of the decision to keep the body where it was: when the tomb was opened to ensure that Gabriel's body was indeed inside, a small cloud rose "from the western peak of the Gran Sasso" and proceeded to drench the area with a "heavy rain." There were between four and seven thousand people present. That same day, there was talk of "at least seven remarkable miraculous happenings," although Gabriel's first miracle was considered to be the healing of the young lady Mary Mazzarelli, an event that took place on October 23rd and about which there was much talk.

Thus, Gabriel would remain definitively in Abruzzi. It had been decided that he was not supposed to go there in the first place, then it was determined that he would have to leave there after arriving, and finally everything had been prepared for him to be taken away after his death: but none of this would take place. God's plan was that he should become an integral part of the people of Abruzzi. In just a few years, he had become an element of their identity and their culture. Gabriel belonged to the people of Abruzzi just as the Gran Sasso belonged to the geography of the region. Can

Abruzzi be imagined without the Gran Sasso? In the same way, neither can it be thought of without Gabriel.

In 1894, the Passionists returned to their House in Isola, next to Gabriel's resting place, whose popularity was rapidly spreading. Father German exclaimed, "Tears were brought to my eyes by the supernatural presence that you could sense at his tomb."

The process of beatification went off without a hitch and was brought to completion in five years. Xavier Tortella, a former servant at the Passionist House, remarked: "If he's not a saint, then no one is." Someone who did not live the best of lives said, "Ever since that little saint left us, my sins have sent shivers down my spine, and I have no desire to indulge in them any more."

On May 31, 1908, Gabriel was officially declared among the blessed by Pius X.

In 1913, *The Echo of Saint Gabriel* came into being, the magazine that made his spirit present to the world.

On May 13, 1920, Gabriel was declared a saint by Benedict XV.

In 1926, he was chosen as co-patron of Italian Catholic youth, and in 1959 was named patron saint of Abruzzi.

In 1973, work began on the construction of his new shrine.

On June 30, 1985, Pope John Paul II made a visit to the shrine and inaugurated the new crypt.

Both Bernard Silvestrelli, Gabriel's fellow student, and Norbert Cassinelli, his director, took part in the beatification ceremony in 1908. Both of them were old men by then and would die three years later, in 1911. As is to be expected, there was a great desire to hear about the life of Gabriel from those who lived with him, and these two eye-witnesses were the center of attention; they were practically living relics of Gabriel. There was a continuous barrage of questions put to the elderly gentlemen whose minds were still sharp: "What was Gabriel like? How did he live? What did he do? Tell us something about him." Bernard sighed and groaned: "That boy has done this to me, he's really done it to me!" Norbert shook his head and, looking off into the distance as if to see him again, said: "That boy did everything with his heart." And then as if to put it in clear focus and expose it to the full light of day, he repeated: "Yes, that's it, he did everything with his heart."

The explanation of Gabriel's spirit, which is still present today, can be found in this last remark of his director: the young man, his heart, his being in love with life in all its stages, first as a layman then as a Passionist.

Whereas the modern society that we have built for ourselves deprives us of our heart, people seek him out precisely because they are drawn to his heart.

"Heart," in the sense that it was lived by Gabriel, means loving people and situations, and giving oneself completely and sincerely to the choices that one has made. It is the capacity to love and to be loved, to understand oneself and others, to stop and think before acting, because certain actions have far-reaching consequences; it means being able to perceive values and to meet God. In this sense, "heart" is conscience, inner life, the depths of one's being.

In today's world, we find that we have grown in all areas: in technology, in material well-being, in our relationship with our world and our planet. We are grasping the deepest secrets of matter, space, and life itself. This is the gift and the boast of our modern age. We cannot go against the path that our Creator has willed for us, he who put into the human heart this irresistible urge for growth. But if progress in science is not accompanied by a like progress in promoting values, growth becomes uneven and erratic. Equilibrium will be lacking, and sooner or later things will fall apart. Marvels of modern technology are wrought by the minds of those who have created them in response to specific challenges, but technological victories can make us blind, even to the point of feeling that we must compete with God himself.

Human development cannot consist solely in technology. Human existence cannot take on the coldness of the mechanical apparatus that technology produces, whether at work, at school, in relationships with others, or even in the creation of new life itself. The human heart cannot be reduced to that level; that is why we must ever defend the heart in all its different manifestations.

If these pages have served to make Gabriel's heart a little bit better understood, then may his example give us the courage not to lose our own hearts or let them be manipulated by others. Doing everything with our heart will help us to find our proper place in the world, and it will help us to make a place for everyone else.

Gabriel is alive because he talks still to his friends, especially to young people. His message always goes from heart to heart.

To learn more about Saint Gabriel of Our Lady of Sorrows, consult the shrine's magazine, *L'Eco di San Gabriele* (*The Echo of Saint Gabriel*) — 64048 S. Gabriele (TERAMO), Italy, published in Italian.

Appendices

Appendix

1. Biographical Data on Gabriel of Our Lady of Sorrows

1838 — March 1: Gabriel is born in Assisi, in the municipal building of the Town Square, and baptized in the Cathedral of Saint Rufinus: his given name is Francis Joseph Vincent Pacific Rufinus, son of Sante Possenti and Agnes Frisciotti; for approximately a year he is in the care of the wet nurse Mrs. Batori, in the district of Petrignano.

1841 — April or May: the family moves to Poggio Mirteto, where his father is named governor;

— November: the family moves to Spoleto, where his father is named legal assessor of the papal delegation;

— December 8: death of his sister Rosa, seven months old, who had remained with her wet nurse in Poggio Mirteto.

1842 — January 26: death of his sister Adele, seven years old, of a cerebral hemorrhage;

— February 9: death of his mother, 41 years old, of meningitis.

1844 — He begins elementary school with the Brothers of the Christian Schools.

1846 — June 1: he is confirmed in the Church of Saint Gregory by the diocesan bishop John Sabbioni.

1848 — October 14: death of his brother Paul, 21 years old, in Chioggia.

1850 — He begins his secondary studies at the Jesuit school in Spoleto.

1851 — June 21: this is the most likely date of his First Holy Communion;

— In the course of a serious throat illness, he promises to become a Religious, but he forgets about the promise as soon as he is better;

— He is outstanding in his humanities studies at school.

1853 — February 13: death of his brother Lawrence, 27 years old, by suicide in Rome;

— His academic successes continue and are consolidated.

1854 — To excess, he gives himself completely to enjoyable pastimes, especially hunting, to the point of causing his father and teachers to worry about him;

— A second serious throat illness and he promises once again to become a Religious; he believes that he has been miraculously cured, he asks to be admitted to the Jesuits, is accepted, but never enters.

1855 — June 7: unexpected death of his sister Mary Louisa, 26 years old;

— August 31: he requests copies of his school records, a sign that some decision is under way.

1856 — April 20 and 23: he receives copies of other school records;

— August 22: he receives an interior locution during the procession with the image of Our Lady: "This life is not made for you"; Our Lady urges him to become a Religious.

— August 24: his confessor Father Charles Bompiani confirms the authenticity of his vocation;

— September 5: he gives a recitation, to a standing ovation, at the Marian school assembly where the academic honors for the Jesuit school in Spoleto are awarded;

— September 6: early in the morning, he leaves Spoleto for Morrovalle, accompanied by his brother Lewis, a Dominican priest;

— September 8: he stops in Loreto where he has an intense interior experience that confirms the decision he has made;

— September 9: he continues the trip from Loreto to the Passionist House in Morrovalle, stopping in Civitanova, with relatives on his mother's side of the

family, and in the countryside of Morrovalle, at the
Capuchin friary where his maternal uncle, Father
John Baptist, is the Superior;

— September 10 - 21: he prepares to enter the novitiate
by going on a spiritual retreat;

— September 21: he begins the novitiate and is vested in
the Passionist habit; he takes the Religious name of
Brother Gabriel of Mary, Our Lady of Sorrows; the
novice master is Father Raphael Ricci, the assistant
novice master Father Norbert Cassinelli.

1857 — September 22: having finished the year of novitiate,
he professes the religious vows as a Passionist.

1858 — He completes his studies of philosophy and Latin;
Father Norbert becomes his spiritual director;

— April: at Fermo he meets his sister Teresa, now
married to Pellegrino Pellegrini, to settle family
business;

— June 20: he is transferred to Pievetorina;

— August: he receives a visit from Pacifica Cucchi, the
Possenti governess;

— September: he receives a visit from his brother
Michael, now a medical student in Rome;

— Another worrisome throat illness.

1859 — He begins his theological training;

— July 4: he begins the trip to Isola del Gran Sasso
where he will continue his studies in preparation for
priesthood; he makes a stop in Recanati, and perhaps
in Torre in Palme, Giulianova, and Montorio al
Vomano;

— July 10: he arrives in Isola del Gran Sasso.

1861 — May 25: he receives tonsure and minor orders in
Penne; this is the first formal step to priesthood;

— From the summer on, his health starts to decline
rapidly;

— November and December: his health continues to
grow worse; he starts to cough up blood; the political

situation does not allow that he be ordained to the priesthood, which would have been difficult in any event because of his precarious health.

1862 — February 27: he dies at 6:30 in the morning.

1868 — Father Paul Bonaccia, a former classmate of Gabriel's and now a canon in Spoleto, publishes the first biography of Brother Gabriel of Our Lady of Sorrows.

1891 — His cause of beatification is introduced.

1892 — October 17 and 18: his body is exhumed in the church of Isola del Gran Sasso.

1908 — May 31: he is officially declared among the blessed by Pius X.

1913 — The magazine entitled, in his honor, *The Echo of Saint Gabriel* begins publication; it now has more than half a million readers.

1920 — May 13: he is officially proclaimed a saint by Benedict XV.

1926 — He is chosen as co-patron of Italian Catholic youth by Pope Pius XI.

1959 — He is named patron saint of Abruzzi by Pope John XXIII.

1973 — Work on his new shrine is begun.

1985 — June 30: Pope John Paul II inaugurates the crypt of the new shrine.

1988 — The 150th anniversary of his birth is celebrated.

2. Bibliographical Information

In this book, all footnotes have been omitted in order to make the reading easier. Nonetheless, the account presented here is solidly based on available sources, from the documentation of the process for beatification to more recent research. Immediately following is an essential select bibliography, presented in chronological order of publication.

P. Bonaccia. *Memorie Storiche sopra la Vita e le Virtù del Giovane Francesco Possenti, tra i Passionisti Confratel Gabriele dell'Addolorata*. Torino: Marietti, 1868.

P. Germano, C.P. *Vita di San Gabriele dell'Addolorata*. Rome: 1924.

P. Gorla. *San Gabriele dell'Addolorata*. Third edition. Caravate: 1951.

P. Ilario, C.P. *Il Santo del Gran Sasso*. Third edition. Santuario San Gabriele: 1962.

B. Ceci. *Scritti di San Gabriele dell'Addolorata*. San Gabriele: Ed. Eco, 1963. 418 pages with a complete bibliography up to the year 1963.

Atti del IX° Convegno di Spiritualità Passionista. "San Gabriele e la Sua Spiritualità." Isola San Gabriele: Direzione dei Convegni di Spiritualità Passionista, 1965.

G. Poage. *Figlio della Passione. San Gabriele dell'Addolorata*. Milan: Editrice Ancora, 1965. 124 pages with bibliography.

N. Cavatassi and F. Giorgini. *Fonti Storico-Biografiche di San Gabriele dell'Addolorata*. San Gabriele: Ed. Eco, 1969. 520 pages.

P. Norberto di Santa Maria, Passionista. *Memorie sulla Vita e Virtù di Confratel Gabriele dell'Addolorata (Francesco Possenti)*. San Gabriele: Ed. Eco, 1970. 254 pages with bibliography.

L. Ravasi. *Sante Possenti. Padre di San Gabriele dell'Addolorata*. Rome: Ed. "Fonti Vive," 1972. 236 pages.

V. Fuente Rodriguez. *San Gabriel de la Dolorosa*. Madrid:
   1973.
F. Pozzi. *San Gabriele dell'Addolorata, Studente Passionista*.
   San Gabriele: Ed. Eco, 1973. 292 pages.
S. Battistelli. *San Gabriele dell'Addolorata, Passionista*. Tenth
   edition. San Gabriele: Editoriale Eco, 1980. 243
   pages.
San Gabriele dell'Addolorata. *Lettere Familiari ed Altri Scritti*.
   Pescara: Editoriale Staurs, 1981. 209 pages; anthol-
   ogy and annotated chronology edited by P. T. Zecca,
   C.P.
F. Piélagos, C.P. *Juventud de Fuego. San Gabriel de la
   Dolorosa*. Barcelona: C.I.P.I., 1981. 124 pages.
C. Sgattoni Gramenzi. *Lavorare col Cuore. San Gabriele
   dell'Addolorata*. Pescara: Editoriale Staurs, 1982.
   101 pages.
P. Bertazzi. *La Ricostruzione di un Modello di Santità: San
   Gabriele dell'Addolorata*. University of Bologna:
   1982.
E. S. Gibert. *Sulle Vette del Gran Sasso. San Gabriele
   dell'Addolorata, Storia e Valori di una Vita*. Pescara:
   Editoriale Staurs, 1983. 222 pages with Italian and
   Spanish bibliography.
Various Authors. *San Gabriele dell'Addolorata e il Suo Tempo.
   Studi, Ricerche e Documentazione*. Edited by T. P.
   Zecca, C.P. Three volumes. San Gabriele: Editoriale
   Eco, 1983, 1986, 1989.
F. D'Anastasio. *Meraviglie di un Santo, Fede di un Popolo*.
   Three volumes. San Gabriele: Editoriale Eco, 1985,
   1987, 1992.
J. C. Delion. *Un Visage de Lumière. Saint Gabriel de
   l'Addolorata*. San Gabriele: Editoriale Eco, 1988.
G. Lenzen. *Gabriel Possenti. Mein Leben ist eine einzige
   Freude*. San Gabriele: Editoriale Eco, 1988.
A. M. C. Conastair. *Possenti. El Hijo del Gubernador*. Buenos
   Aires: Ocruxaves, 1989.
E. Annibali. *La Madonna della Quercia di Morrovalle ed i
   Passionisti*. San Gabriele: Editoriale Eco, 1990.